Early Praise for *From Fired to Fabulous*

“Beth Solomon’s *From Fired to Fabulous* brilliantly reframes the experiences around being fired. As someone working in HR and a career coach at a major university, I see employees often struggle with the emotional toll of job loss. Solomon provides the tools and mindset shift needed to turn those challenges into opportunities. FF2Fis an extremely valuable resource for professionals at any stage of their careers.”

— Shayna Hodges, human resources executive,
University of Maryland

“A must-read for anyone in the workforce, *From Fired to Fabulous* will entertain, inspire, and equip you to more successfully navigate the ups and downs of your career.”

— Alison Cardy, executive coach, author of *Career Grease, How to Get Unstuck and Pivot Your Career*

“You can read this book as a self-help, a how-to, a comfort soother or simply as great entertainment. Whether you’re searching for your next job or your first, Beth Solomon is a great storyteller — you won’t be disappointed.”

— Kate Lehrer, author and panelist, *National Public Radio’s* Diane Rehm Book Club

“Resilience. Grit. *Ganas.* Beth Solomon’s book describes how to recover from one of the worst days of your career and take crucial steps to find your dream job. With wit and wisdom, Solomon describes the mindset you’ll need and steps to land a position that’s a good fit for your passion, values and financial security. It’s also an entertaining read! As a friend once told me, ‘If you’re not fired at least a few times in your life, you’re doing something wrong!’”

— Dianne Saenz, media executive

"Perceptive, empathetic, vulnerable, hilarious, and action-oriented... my favorite kind of entertaining read. I was locked in to her story while learning from her authentic experience."

— Melanie Minzes, humanitarian organization leader

"What a brilliant idea to fill a glaring hole in today's professional work world."

— Didi Cutler, photographer, lecturer, and columnist for *The Georgetowner*

"Beth has created chicken soup for the professional soul in this raw, refreshingly candid guidebook on how to bounce back stronger than ever. We could all learn from her incredible resiliency."

— Robie Mitchell, CAPM, development executive

From FIRED to FABULOUS

How to Turn Professional Fiascos into your Launch Pad to Success

BETH SOLOMON

ISBN:

Layout and Cover Design: Cheakina

Table of Contents

Also by Beth Solomon

Georgetown Dish

For my sweet mother, who made me who I am, and for Gero, the love of my life

"Life is a daring adventure, or nothing."

Hellen Keller

Preface

"I just came from a small lunch of my Clinton White House coworkers. As we went around the table and updated everyone about what we were now doing, I was struck by how many women did not talk about being laid off or fired from jobs. Even though some of us at the table knew that was the case. Everything was always woven into a story of how they chose to do something different. We need to change the conversation so that we can all say proudly 'I got laid off' or 'I was fired from that job.'"

— former White House staffer

Introduction

I've been fired. A lot. In fact, I've been fired more times than anyone I know. I used to be embarrassed by my history, but then I noticed a story hidden under that pile of pink slips. We don't talk about losing our jobs much. Doing so makes us feel ashamed, rejected, sometimes humiliated, or even worthless — a disappointment to our families. But the truth is, just because you're doing a good job, you're talented, you're dedicated, and you're smart, doesn't mean you won't be downsized, dismissed, passed over for a promotion, demoted, or just plain fired. Rather than being hurt, I've come to realize that getting fired can literally be — and often is — one of the best things that's ever happened to you.

I attended excellent public schools, graduated from an Ivy-covered college, and could afford graduate courses thanks to my parents' unwavering support. Education was emphasized as a priority in our home. My dear mother helped us with homework and made sure we learned how to write. Growing up in leafy Bethesda, Md., in such a supportive family was a huge head start in life.

And yet, I've been fired many times throughout my career. Losing my job was always financially terrifying, despite all my advantages. Finding myself suddenly terminated, pushed out, or having my job "eliminated" ran over my ego like a tank, leaving its tracks behind like scars.

But the experience made me stronger. And better. The truth is, we all need to be ready to lose our jobs, prepare for the inevitable professional bumps and bruises, and understand that getting fired can be a powerful catapult to a better life.

In *From Fired to Fabulous,* I draw on my personal experiences — as an executive headhunter (I was forced out), bank vice president (terminated) and Hollywood talent agency associate (resigned fairly gracefully) as well as many more — to offer a detailed roadmap to turn common professional fiascoes into better jobs, higher compensation, and a more fulfilling career.

Each chapter combines hair-raising true stories from the professional battlefield with practical advice on how to react and recover quickly — starting from the moment the axe falls, to the morning after, through the initial grieving period, to the resume rewrite, negotiating severance, to personal and online networking tips, tricks, and strategies. I then describe in detail how to establish the essential habits to build long-term financial security and snag career opportunities that fuel your soul.

The pandemic of 2020-2022 accelerated trends that were shaping the workplace already. Remote work increased physical isolation from colleagues and mentors. For many, technology became the primary means of daily interaction and connection — as well as an increasingly potent replacement for humans. The resulting interchangeability of employees in many roles has led to inherent workplace instability — creating a vicious cycle. In short, we all need to adjust and build new job-hunting and career navigation skills — exactly what you will find in this book.

Work is a gift. It is a vehicle that lets us bring our skills and talents into the world. It should be fulfilling. Some days, it should be joyous! Each and every day, work should be eye-opening. This book is designed to help you recover from the inevitable career nosedives and embarrassing belly flops to pop back above the surface and reach your next safe, sandy beach, where you can sparkle again in the sun.

You're Fired! Now What?

As a black sky faded to cool indigo on a late-May morning in Washington, D.C., I yawned, jumped out of bed, and buttoned on my favorite robin's-egg-blue pantsuit before sprinting to a pre-dawn workout at a gym near my office.

After a quick shower, hair styled, make-up on, I ducked through the glass doors of our local French café chain, seeing a smiling face behind the counter. "*Commo esta Usted?*" Blanca called out over piles of croissants, bagels, fruit, and spreads under the glass case between us.

"Could I have six of these, six of those, butter, and cream cheese for all?" I asked excitedly.

"Are you having a party?" Blanca asked, punching in my big order on her screen.

"My bosses are here for a meeting," I nodded, rechecking my list to make sure I had thought of everything.

"*Buena suerte!*" she called, touching her heart to wish me luck.

Racing down the sidewalk as the rising sun shot spears of light between the tall downtown office buildings, I pushed open our glass workspace door and propped my sunglasses on the top of my head, smiling at the sight of Heather and Kendra, two of my young teammates, at their desks already in our cool loft space, working away. I was proud of them and knew my bosses, the board members, would be impressed at the look and feel of this active beehive.

The board chair, vice chair, and treasurer would be arriving at our open office in half an hour. They had requested the meeting. I wasn't sure of the exact purpose, but it was about time to discuss next year's budget, and, after a glowing annual performance review, I had asked for a raise.

Surveying the tasty spread on our conference table with the gurgle of brewing coffee in the background, I looked at the clock, eager for the show to begin.

It was 8:59.

A pale face surrounded by curly auburn hair appeared in the entrance door window. I held the door with a big smile as first the chair, Susan, the vice chair, Jana, and the treasurer, Mort, filed in, peeling off their light jackets in the warmth of our loft-style, sunny space.

"How are you, Mort?" I shook the treasurer's hand warmly and showed the group into the adjoining conference room. "Coffee? Tea? What can I get you?"

I had reason to be looking forward to this meeting. A year and a half earlier, the board had hired me as CEO of this small trade association (a nonprofit corporation) which they said needed a massive turnaround. The previous CEO had been in his position for 25 years, doing less and less work as time went on, and, in an ongoing feud with the board, had let revenues slow to a trickle while bills poured in, creating a sea of red ink. When I started the job, the organization's offices were burrowed inside a termite-infested Virginia townhouse. The roof leaked onto random cast-off metal desks covered with dusty stacks of old mail, surrounded by scratched and broken chairs and musty boxes full of files. Flying termites and the smell of mold filled the air, the ceilings strung with cobwebs.

"YOUR STATUS UNDER CODE 501(C) 3 WILL BE REVOKED IN 14 DAYS," screamed a warning letter from the U.S. Department of Justice — just one of the legal problems facing the neglected organization. The website looked like a 1970s Ford Pinto overturned in a ditch, weeds growing in it, not drivable. Nobody knew how much money the organization had in the bank, because its former accountant had moved to Florida and couldn't be reached.

The staff had mostly run for the hills in recent years. By the time I started, only one employee remained, and she was *very* angry.

So, I got to work.

Flipping my laptop open in various Starbucks and then in a tiny borrowed office in downtown Washington, I hired a respected accounting firm to straighten out the books. A few hardworking board members and I together paid the taxes and filed documents to regain legal operating status with the IRS and Justice Department. I then recruited and onboarded a small team of talented colleagues, rolled out new educational programming for members which boosted conference attendance to record highs, which generated new revenue, prominence, media coverage, and the first budget surplus in years. I was riding high. Things were going so well after the first 14 months, that I had asked for a raise to bring my compensation in line with my peers leading similar organizations. Honestly, I was earning a good salary, but the fact that my compensation was 30-40 percent less than my peers in the male-dominated financial industry seemed like another problem that needed fixing for the long-term good of everyone.

Maybe the board leaders would have good news on that front, I thought. Almost in unison, Susan, Jana and Mort put their bags down, sat down in our conference room, scooted their chairs forward and pulled out their laptops and papers. Susan slowly lifted a tea cup to her lips and set it down without a sound.

Mort looked at me and said, "Beth, shut the door."

A little abrupt, I thought. But Mort was a tough ex-banker from Brooklyn. I jumped up to close the door and sat back down.

Susan opened the file folder in front of her. Her fingers were trembling. She started reading a prepared statement on several pages which shook in her hands so loudly you could hear the flapping, like bird's wings. "The board of directors of the National Business Investment Association met on May 15, and with a quorum of 16 members present, voted to terminate your employment, effective today," she said, looking down.

A rock dropped into my stomach.

Susan's voice was getting quieter, like a car driving away. She cleared her throat and touched her temple. As if using all the breath she could muster to force the words out, she said, "The board has voted for a reasonable severance payment and would like you to review and sign this separation agreement." She looked up at the wall, then down again. Jana, the vice chair, was staring at her lap. "You can take your things home with you or we can have them boxed up," Susan said.

Huh? Was I watching a movie? Was this real?

Mort sat there, tapping on his iPad keyboard, his lips pressed closed. "Do you have any questions?" Susan asked, not looking up.

A million thoughts raced through my head as Susan trembled through the legalese. I looked straight at her, then the others. A few seconds felt like an hour.

"Why?" I asked them simply. *Why?* That was the question I had.

Susan looked at the others and then at me. "We've decided to go in a different direction," she repeated.

"OK," I managed. "Did I do something wrong?"

Susan threw a glance at the treasurer. Mort looked up from his keyboard to stare at the industrial ceiling. With a mechanical buzz, the air conditioner under the window started to blow again, breaking the dead silence. "We've decided to go in a different direction," Susan repeated, following a script.

"I understand," I said. "But I'd like to know if this is about something I did."

"It's not, Beth," said Jana, almost in a pleading voice, looking at me for the first time, "but we've decided to go in a different direction." This conversation was going nowhere.

I knew I had to decide quickly what to say and do, overriding the confusion and fear coursing through my veins. "May I talk with my team?" I stammered. "I would like them to hear this from me," came the words from my mouth. I wanted to spare my young colleagues some of the shock I was feeling, and to reassure them through this chaos.

Susan and Mort looked at each other. "Your team has left the building."

©Glasbergen

MY TEAM HAS LEFT THE BUILDING? I yelped inside. Weird was getting weirder. My head was spinning. But even in that moment, as I absorbed the news of my assassination, listening to the drone of human resources gobbledegook that has become the hallmark of modern-day terminations, another channel in my brain lit up, like a bright flare in the middle of a dark sea night. *This is ridiculous,* said a quiet voice inside my head. *These* people *are ridiculous. Beth, you are going to be OK.*

Raising her head timidly from behind her tea cup, Susan repeated, "You can clean out your desk now or we can have your belongings boxed and shipped." I looked over at my bright white desk reflecting a streak of sun from the window. I looked at all the matching white IKEA desks that the team and I had built ourselves. I looked at the beautiful industrial ceiling, and the empty chairs of my co-workers. My heart was palpitating, but I didn't want to run out of the room. I needed a moment to try to think clearly.

"Um, I can take care of my desk now," I said.

The board members stood up, tapped on their phones, leaned on chairs around the conference table, murmuring in low tones as I gingerly stacked my laptop, framed photos, a few books, a hairbrush, mirror, and extra headphones into a couple of shopping bags. Sweeping my belongings off my desk into the bags — even as my executioners watched — felt liberating somehow.

By the time I had gathered up all the artifacts of my *suddenly former* job, a half-smile had returned to my face. As I said good-bye and wished them luck, my smile brightened. I think I even said, "If there's anything I can do to be of help, please let me know!" My game face was holding, as if superglued. Part of me couldn't believe the cheery words coming from my mouth. But at least I wasn't crying.

What I was thinking was:

Oh my God.

I can't believe this.

Stay calm, Beth. Don't let them see your fear.

F-ing idiots.

What am I going to do???

* * *

Lugging the shopping bags filled with the remains of my ex-job, I pushed myself through the revolving doors of the building to the sidewalk. A few heavy drops of rain smacked the pavement and my face. Looking for shelter, I ducked into a parking garage, leaned my bags against a bare cement wall, straightened my shoulders, and called our PR firm.

"Hey!" Lauren picked up the phone on the first ring, her voice cheery.

"Guess what," I said, holding my abdomen. "They fired me."

"Who? What?"

"Susan, Jana, the board. They just told me. They asked me to clear out my desk."

"Wha???" she said, "You're shitting me."

"I'm serious," I said, twisting my heel into the cement. My voice echoed eerily down the ramp to the underground parking.

"I can't *believe* this!" Lauren said. Her firm had generated unprecedented national media coverage for us, leading to climbing membership, sponsorships, and revenue for the association. A firehose of epithets followed. "Fucking morons! Scumbags! They've lost their minds!" Her words lifted my spirits, firing at my detractors like the heavy pellets of rain pounding the cement outside. I stood up straighter for a moment, then slumped.

As the clouds let loose a monsoon-like downpour, I flagged a taxi. The Ethiopian driver's kind eyes appeared in his rear view mirror as he asked me how my day was going. The only words I could think of spilled out of my mouth: "I just got fired."

"Ohhhhhhhh," he said. Simply, "Ohhhhhhhh." The wipers' rhythmic *thud-squeak-thud* stood in for further conversation as we drove the 15 minutes to my house.

Dropping the shopping bags as I came through the front door of my beloved old D.C. brownstone, I trod upstairs and slowly peeled off my dampened "good-luck" robin's-egg-blue suit, hanging it out to dry. I climbed into bed and stared at the ceiling, listening to the heavy rain slapping my windows.

* * *

Nick was standing against a doric column at the beautiful bar of Joe's Stone Crab, taking a sip of an amber Manhattan, when I strode in. Seeing me, he leaned in for a hug. The bar was crowded. The restaurant had a weeks-long waiting list.

"What can I get you?" he asked over the din.

"I'd like a glass of really good Chardonnay," I said loudly. Then quietly, "Because…I…got…fired today."

Nick's jaw dropped. He stared back at me, his thumb hooked through the belt loop of his Levi's under an expensive-looking blazer. His sturdy shoulders reassured me.

We had arranged this dinner date weeks ago. Nick was CEO of a large hotel company. I had met him when he was chairman of the board of my previous organization where I was a VP. Nick was a *real* CEO. A model of professional success — respected, super smart, fun, wealthy, and *single,* like me.

Since I had started my new position a year and a half ago, he had been in touch to meet for dinner. Our calendars were both full of travel and meetings, but eventually — ironically — we set the date for this night. Looking at the ceiling from my bed in the afternoon, I thought,

Should I even go? Will it be too difficult? Should I call and cancel?

I admired Nick. I had always wanted to be a CEO. *Once you're a CEO, you never go back,* I thought. Meaning, *you never have to go back to being a mere* vice president, *a regular old* executive. I believed my first CEO assignment would be a ticket to more prestige, travel, interesting people, travel, compensation, and fun.

In several interviews during the search process, including lunch with the chair and a panel interview of eight board members, the job at the National Business Investment Association sounded challenging and exciting. They told me I would inherit a broken organization, a small nonprofit on life support. I had started businesses before and loved creating, fixing, and building things. The board members wanted a total overhaul, which I knew would require a lot of change and invention. New people, lots to do, the need to reinvent the brand — all of this had sounded inviting to me.

"Are you OK?" Nick asked, leaning his head toward me at the bar. "I would be curled up in a ball if that had happened to me this morning."

The ice-cold white burgundy slid across my tongue like an Arctic river cooling the Sahara. I tilted my head up at the tall marble columns around us. "I think I'm fine," I smiled, nodding slowly. "It's been an interesting day."

*   *   *

As if in a dream, flutes of champagne bubbled as we nibbled on cool Alaskan crab legs.

"I'm treating tonight," Nick announced, as the waiter reached our booth in the corner. "We're celebrating." Nick's thick salt-and-pepper hair was neatly trimmed, reaching the collar of his light blue button-down shirt.

"I got fired today," I smiled, running my fingers across the cloth napkin in my lap. I didn't have the energy to pretend.

Our waiter froze. His dark eyelashes fluttered sympathetically in the pause. "You're in the right place now," he said, soothingly. "Let me pour you another glass."

Nick wanted to hear all the details and threw plenty of verbal grenades at the perpetrators. A few glasses in, I felt like I was telling a great war story, though still in shock from the battle.

"Have you ever been fired?" I asked him, slurping an oyster with a lemon juice spike.

"Of course. Hasn't everybody?" Nick raised his eyebrows and shook his head, topping off our glasses. "It happens to the best of us," he winked.

Nick and I traded stories like old war buddies late into the night. When at one point I finally started to cry, Nick held my chilly hand between both of his. "Don't cry, Beth," he said softly. "You've done nothing wrong, you're so talented and strong, and you're going to be just fine. Trust me on this one." After a hug in front of the restaurant, Nick tucked me into a taxi home, where I flopped onto my bed and tried to sleep.

Memories swirled in my brain. When I had been fired from a large trade association several years earlier, I had been even more upset. Hired as a strategic communications consultant to the CEO, I was promoted to a full-time position as senior vice president six months later. But four months after that, the day before I was going on summer vacation, the head of HR and his assistant dropped by my office.

"Do you have a few minutes?" the human resources chief asked.

As I noticed Melvin's brown suit, beige shirt, and dark green tie, a thought bubble floated by that such a visit was unusual, but in weird work situations, the best course is usually to be polite and act normal. "Sure! Come on in, Melvin," I said, rolling in an extra chair from the empty office next door for Melvin and his assistant Jada, who stood a statuesque 5'10" on her mauve stilettos. I was in a good mood, getting ready to leave for my first vacation since I had started the job. As they sat down, the grim looks on their faces told me Melvin and Jada were not just "saying hello."

" The good news is that the rest of your day will seem wonderful compared to this. "

cartoonstock.com

"We're very sorry, Beth, but your position is being eliminated," Melvin said.

"MY POSITION IS BEING ELIMINATED?" I repeated, an octave higher. "But it's a new position. You just created it!" I said. "I've only been in this job four months!"

"James is going to be taking over communications, and the association won't need your position anymore," he said with a shrug. "Dionne (the CEO) wanted to be here to tell you herself, but she had another commitment."

I was swooning inside but trying to keep my cool. This was going to be a stain on my resume. *A Big Black Eye.*

"Nothing to worry about. We'll figure out the details when you get back from vacation," chirped Jada.

NOTHING TO WORRY ABOUT? WE'LL FIGURE OUT THE DETAILS WHEN I'M BACK FROM VACATION???

My face turned hot. What vacation? How was I going to take a vacation knowing I was losing my job???

This is cruel, I thought. Digging my fingernails into my thigh behind my wood-toned Formica desk, I tried not to sound angry. "I understand," I managed. "Dionne has the right to have the team she wants." I think I said that a few times as my mind raced. *How should I handle this?* "But the optics are going to be terrible on my resume," I pleaded. "I haven't even been here a year." I scanned their faces for clues. Part of me was trying to figure out what really happened, while part of me was trying to figure out what to say.

"You'll get some severance," Melvin said. "I'll send you some documents to sign."

Where was Dionne, the CEO? Why was this really happening? I yelped inside. *Keep cool, Beth. And think about what you need to say right now,* I silently commanded myself.

"Everything is going to be fine," Jada went on cheerfully. "Take some time to think during your vacation, and we'll work everything out when you return."

Yeah right, I thought.

Somehow, the fact that my boss didn't have the guts to tell me herself felt like an extra kick in the stomach. My status was reduced to hearing the worst news I could possibly receive at work from *nonchalant* surrogates.

Later, during a stressful "vacation" with my parents at a house they had rented in Maine, I put the pieces together. At least I think I did.

Another new senior executive, the executive vice president, had used inappropriate sexual words and body language toward one of his female deputies on several occasions. She reported it to me, and I then reported it to Dionne, the CEO, and the chairman of the board. Dionne thanked me — and required "Greg" to attend a day-long sexual harassment and behavior management training session. A month later, my position was eliminated.

While I felt humiliated, upset, and even frightened, I later realized the events which followed were fairly typical. Dionne's leadership team had experienced constant churn since her arrival as CEO. Dionne couldn't afford to lose Greg, who served in the most important position in the company next to the CEO. To save Greg, Dionne axed me as the sacrificial lamb.

Then, my phone started ringing. Board members who heard what happened were upset. They started calling their friends. One board member in particular, a former chairman of the organization, was livid about my sudden departure. He told me he was calling other CEOs he knew who would love to have me on their teams.

"Gerry, I'm really lucky that when I fall down, I have friends like you to help me back up on my feet," I said, panting slightly as I walked uphill during yet another daytime run to Safeway from an English basement apartment in which I lived at the time. "You have not fallen down!" Gerry exclaimed. "You've just stubbed your toe and you're going to keep on walking!"

Within the month, a CEO Gerry had contacted hired me as a strategy consultant, which would turn into the best executive role of my life. In fact, Dionne's dumping of me generated new fans and friendships which helped take my career to new heights — over and over — in the years to come.

No Shame

"When you have shame, you don't share it." [1]

Billie Jean King

My 51-year-old husband "left" his senior role at X four years ago, and he hasn't worked since.

Manu, executive headhunter

Getting fired gutted my self-confidence. I was never the same. It affected the rest of my life. It still does.

Dean, former hospital accountant

They said my tone in supervising staff was "off" and that I need to take a break. My tone is no different from my male colleagues. I think I'm getting forced out, but they won't tell me what's happening. I can't sleep at night.

Valerie, political organizer

I shouldn't have complained to HR about my new boss's harassing comments. I'm sure that's why I got laid off in the re-org.

Jamal, media relations director

In 1971, our family moved to Washington, D.C., after my dad's three-year assignment in New Delhi, India, with the State Department. We lived in a compact brick colonial perched on a hill about five blocks from the elementary school where I had started first grade. One day, I told my mom I wanted to walk to school by myself.

I was six years old, but Mom had always encouraged my independence. She bent down in her 1970s red-and-white checkered peddle-pushers to look me in the eye encouragingly. "Do you think you know the way, Beth?"

"Of course!" I said.

"Well sure then," she said warily.

From that time on, in the mornings, I would walk down the alley behind our house to get to the crosswalk where the older "safety patrols" wore orange reflective belts and helped us grammar schoolers cross the intersection to school. My mother told me years later that she would secretly follow me on my walks to school, not letting me see her, so I could feel that I was independent and accomplishing this by myself while she secretly watched over me.

One day after the final bell rang at 3:00, I was skipping down the sidewalk towards home, in my own world. I loved first grade, and I loved going home where a snack would be waiting, as well as "Mister Roger's Neighborhood," my favorite TV show.

Lost in my own happy thoughts, I suddenly heard shouting. At first it was distant, miles away from my peaceful daydream. Then, like a roaring monster, a big sixth-grade boy wearing an orange patrol belt yelled in my face at the top of his lungs. "WAAALKK!!!" he screamed. "WWALLKKK!!!"

I hadn't realized I was skipping (not walking) through the

crosswalk, which had turned this sixth-grader into a bellowing Vesuvius. Was I breaking a rule? He shouted,"DEMERIT!!!" I didn't know what that meant, but I knew it was bad. Feeling ashamed, I said nothing, and slowed instantly to a walk. Eager to get away from him, I scrambled quickly up the hill back to the house. Mom was outside laying bricks in sand to form a new pathway in the back yard.

"Hi honey!" she beamed, brushing the loose strands of hair out of her face and the sand off her fingers, as she turned toward me in a squat. "How was school today?" I tried to talk, but instead, hot tears like a river of molten lava flooded my eyes and cheeks. I threw my little arms around her and collapsed into sobs.

"What's the matter?" she pleaded. "What happened, Beth???"

"I was...He...." I couldn't get more than a few words out without dissolving into hot tears.

Trying to catch my breath, I explained how the safety patrol screamed at me at in the crosswalk, yelling so loudly, the whole neighborhood could hear. At six, I was embarrassed, I was ashamed. Frightened. Humiliated. I felt completely powerless and helpless. I hadn't realized I was doing anything wrong, just skipping down the sidewalk. But I had unknowingly broken the rules (at least the rules the sixth-grade patrol had decided to enforce that day). Had I been 10 or 12, I might have yelled back, "Shut up!" or "YOU walk!," but my first-grader self was intimidated and scared. The scene remains burned into my memory.

In the next years, I was spanked by my father at age seven or eight for not coming home before dark, as I was instructed to do. I still remember the burning shame of having to pull down my pants, and the sting of the slaps on my bottom.

When we're fired, or passed over, or even reprimanded at work — if we're not careful — we can unconsciously re-experience our first encounters with humiliation and shame. Reliving those emotions can be extreme and can last weeks, months, or years, if we're not alert to the dynamic. Those original experiences of humiliation lurk in our sub-consciences like hibernating snakes. Getting fired, passed over or not chosen can revive those vipers instantly. Their venom flows through our emotional veins like poison, weakening us, debilitating us, hammering our egos, and even sapping our physical energy. The new rejection affirms the deep-seated fear that we're truly NOT good enough, we never will be, and we deserve this rejection.

"He Replied All."

cartoonstock.com

But wait. It is *we* who make *ourselves* miserable by feeling old wounds patched over by scar tissue. *We punish ourselves* at the exact moment we need to feel confident, strong, and attractive — to secure our next job.

Why do we do this? Psychologists say the unconscious mind forms before birth, while the conscious mind forms much later. Experiences that shaped our minds in our early years, if left unexamined, can leave scars that trigger behavior and extreme reactions years later if we don't examine and resolve them. We unconsciously repeat the emotional experience of our earliest years — rather than quickly flicking off the attack on our egos and building ourselves back up.

When I was fired the first time, part of the reason the experience was so humiliating was that I felt six years old again, getting yelled at by the safety patrol, or spanked for coming home after dark. A disappointment to my family. A "public" failure. The first time I was let go (from a waitressing job in a sleepy New York coffee shop), I didn't even tell anyone.

Little kids are too young to distinguish between justified and unjustified punishment. They simply feel terrible. A young girl who is punished by her parents knows she has disappointed the people on whom she literally depends for survival. It doesn't matter that the punishment may have happened because Dad was in a bad mood, or Mom was stressed about finances.

When we get fired or passed over, we feel stupid. We feel helpless. Even worthless. We replay scenes and encounters from work over and over in our minds, like forensic investigators, wondering which conversation went wrong, at what point so-and-so turned against us, how we should have handled this meeting or that presentation differently.

But self-questioning and self-criticism in these moments are usually not helpful. Feeling ashamed for an extended period is DEFINITELY not recommended. Why? For one thing, self-flagellation is probably not justified. News flash: the workplace is not fair. Often, it's not even rational. It's just a set of people with all the good and bad qualities of any group of human beings. Many of your colleagues are insecure. Some of them likely want to hang on, so they can keep paying their bills, because they can't (or think they can't) get the positions they really want. So if you're leading change, or — heaven forbid — being innovative, you can unwittingly threaten individuals and whip up an active movement to oust you. The workplace organism, having identified you as a threat, will surround you like an amoeba and crush you.

If you have lost your job, been passed over, or can't get a job you want, you may feel hurt or rejected. But remember, the workplace isn't *just* or equitable. Instead, it's full of petty jealousy, politics, and predation. Rather than looking at job loss with regret, look at the opportunity that comes with it. Because getting terminated or losing your job gives you a chance to make a bigger change than someone who is employed.

That's harsh, you say! I'm not pretending that losing your job is easy. Getting fired is usually financially frightening, no matter how well prepared you are. Being unemployed is *stressful*. But studies show this: *changing jobs is the way to increase your salary faster than staying in the same job.* In fact, staying put can hold your compensation *down.* Research shows that remaining employed at a company for longer than two years will decrease your lifetime earnings by up to 50 percent (!). [2] That's because while professional employees who stay at the same company can generally expect a 3% annual raise (when times are good), changing jobs will generally snag you a 10 to 20 percent increase in your salary. According to a 2022 Pew Research Center analysis, half of workers who changed jobs saw their pay increase nearly 10%. The median worker who stayed put saw an inflation-adjusted loss of almost 2%.[3]

Example: Malika managed the $40 million corporate grants portfolio of a large international development nonprofit. Over 12 years, her team grew to nine direct reports — she was responsible for 90% of the corporate donations the nonprofit received. Year after year, Malika received excellent performance reviews and scheduled salary increases. When a more junior person was hired at a salary 20% higher than Malika's to do business development, she was angry. When that person failed year after year to bring in 1% of the funds Malika raised, she became increasingly bitter.

Malika was experiencing a career reality: often, employers spend more on new hires and don't reward employees who stay. Why? Because they think they don't have to. Longterm employees may be perceived as unlikely to leave. That puts them at a disadvantage when compensation and bonuses are divvied out.

Besides more money, a new role at a different organization typically expands your skills, and thus, your value. "There are great stories of people who have switched companies or industries and have been able to grow their careers way faster than they would have at the original company," said Lauren McGoodwin, the founder of career-development service Career Contessa.[4]

In short, losing your job builds strength and resilience, can *improve* your chances of rising in your career, helps you gain new experiences and skills, and puts you on track to making more money.

While it always makes sense to learn from mistakes and improve, spending too much time analyzing what happened right after you have been fired, passed over for a promotion, or denied a new job can simply be a form of self-torture rather than a source of wisdom. The best response is to flick off the bad feelings, let yourself recover, and start to rebuild your confidence and excitement to meet the opportunities that are about to open ahead.

"Think of this as an opportunity. All those great contests employees are ineligible to win...well, now you're eligible."

cartoonstock.com

As hard as the experience is, you have to keep reminding yourself that you have been *liberated* to find a better opportunity. You have been freed. This is not to make light of the financial and emotional burdens that add to the pressure. You need to be *prepared*. (We'll cover financial strategies and security in Chapter 9.)

For months and even a year or two after I was terminated from my first CEO role, I agonized. I asked people who were involved with the organization if they knew why I was fired. Most said the association just wasn't ready for the change they said they wanted. But I wondered how I had lost the support of the board and worried that I had done something they thought was wrong. "No, Beth. It really wasn't anything you did," one board member told me a year later. "One of the upcoming chairmen wanted things *his* way and over time the board simply went along with him. Nobody thought you did anything wrong. Not at all."

My dear mother said it best — and almost immediately — at the time. "Beth," she said, "you knew that place was never a fit. And they treated you pretty well on your way out the door." What she meant was, I had never been thrilled with the board or the industry. I often complained to my family and friends. And when the nonprofit gave me my walking papers, I received a severance package equal to six-months' compensation, when I had only served 18 months.

Had I been offered the role as a two-year assignment in which I would be paid to take off the last six months, I would have said, "Where do I sign?!" I would have planned a sabbatical with exotic travel. I would have been delighted to turn the keys back to the board and not have to deal with 25 bosses for six months with full pay and benefits. I would have seen the brief assignment as a great opportunity.

This, I believe, is the way to think about all job losses and missed opportunities. Unless you stole something, didn't perform, abused or acted inappropriately with colleagues, the factual explanation for termination is that you and the organization were no longer a good fit. Being denied a job you wanted can be even more frustrating, in a way, because you may have started imagining and planning for the new role without experiencing the day-to-day humdrum of most assignments.

Getting fired or passed over, depending on the circumstances, is a *badge of honor* — a reflection of your talent and uniqueness. Getting fired or getting passed over is, in fact, a precious gift. In a decade of jobs that included a demotion, getting forced out, having my position "eliminated" (legal cover for "we want you out") and an outright termination, my compensation increased four-fold — 400%. And each job was better than the last in crucial ways.

Getting up off the ground immediately afterward is the hardest part!

Exercise: Tracing Painful Emotions Back to Their Roots

In the *Harvard Business Review,* Joseph Genny has written that early childhood experiences cause the most primal part of our brains "to code certain conditions as threatening — physically or psychically. And from that point forward, you don't get to vote on whether you'll react when those conditions are present," including at work.[5]

Close your eyes and breathe deeply. Settle into long breaths and relax your muscles, starting with your toes and ankles, going up through your body to your neck. Relax your face.

Now, think of a time you were told your position was being eliminated, or you didn't get chosen for a job. Relive the scene in your mind. Check the sensations in your body. How does your stomach feel when you remember? Are you feeling any other physical sensations? Are you taking long breaths, or have they shortened? Experience again what it felt like physically and emotionally to hear such dreaded news.

Now, as if going backward in the river of your life to your earliest memories, try to remember the first time you felt these physical sensations.

Emotions are like the strings of a guitar in your being. They vibrate from end to end, so you can trace an emotion you feel now back to the first time you felt it — the vibration is carried along the string.

You may need to sit for a while. Breathe deeply. Take an emotional elevator down in time to your earliest memories. Try to remember what was happening when you felt these physical sensations. Who was with you? What was said? How old were you? Was it light or dark? Inside or outside?

What is the sensation you feel in your body?

Sit with that memory for a while. Describe to yourself the sensations you feel physically.

You may think of a few childhood scenes in which you felt similar physical sensations to those you experienced when you lost your job or weren't hired. Write them down in a journal. Describe your feelings to a friend.

Now that you know that those early experiences of shame and feeling worthless are lurking beneath your current consciousness, able to stamp out your happiness, optimism and self-confidence, you can slay them. Once identified, these emotional vampires are no longer in control. You can keep them as pets, but now *you* are in charge.

From Fired to Fabulous: First Steps Forward

The first morning I woke up as a fired CEO, my head was throbbing. The revelry and war-story-telling of the night before with my friend Nick, fueled by a deluge of wine, exacted a morning-after price. I felt like a cadaver in a boat, tossing in stormy seas. Limping out on my terrace, I phoned my mentor, Philip, the leading attorney in the industry in which I had last worked. A tall, elegant man with many Ivy League degrees, Philip had worked for U.S. presidents and advised Senators and countless CEOs. Somehow, he also found time for me — supporting me professionally, advising me, treating me almost like a daughter. As painful as it was, I had to tell him. After clearing my throat a zillion times and somehow stumbling through the bloody truth, I mentioned the 10-page separation agreement my former employers wanted me to accept. I heard silence on the end of the line.

"You didn't sign it, did you?" Philip intoned in his deep, principled voice, after an eternal pause. I hadn't. Philip sighed. He gave me the name of a lawyer. In his noble baritone, Philip tried to be reassuring, but he sounded concerned.

"Those bastards!" my friend Bill, another mentor, also a top Washington attorney, thundered. "They didn't deserve you, Beth. They are pathetic!!!"

Bill introduced me to the partner-in-charge of the employment practice at his law firm. Paying for a top lawyer wasn't cheap, but a necessary investment in securing more money in my severance package. The attorney asked me to call my former boss, the board chair, to let her know he would be calling her, or whether the organization preferred to work through a lawyer he should contact.

I had to steel myself to call Susan. I was so angry at her, and so hurt. How could she have done this? She had recruited me. She knew how hard I had worked. There had been no warning, no heads up. My face stung as I sat on the terrace under a flame-throwing morning sun. The hangover, the flood of emotions, made me feel bruised all over, like I'd been in a car accident.

But I knew expressing anger at Susan wasn't good strategy if I wanted to negotiate the best possible deal for my exit. At this point, I was hoping for a bit of sympathy in the situation and to bring out the board's better angels. So, in the best business-like, pre-firing, friendly voice I could muster, I called Susan to let her know that I would be working with an attorney and politely requested an emailed copy of the draft separation agreement.

Susan was cordial on the phone. Always business-like, she didn't convey any emotion, but I thought I heard a tone of empathy in her voice. As the chair, she had been the one, technically, to terminate me, but I started to feel that canning me might not have been her idea.

Such a possibility injected a little relief into my aching body. Susan readily agreed to email me the legal document, I told her the name of my attorney, and we hung up. I exhaled, relieved to have completed that task.

Now what?

I didn't want to stay in my house all day. Slowly I got dressed, folded some scattered clothes from the night before, and found dark sunglasses to hide my swollen face.

The Big Bear Café around the corner had an outdoor area with trellises of grape vines overhead. Sitting at a wooden table under the dappled shade of the late morning sun, I took a sip of an iced latte, whose $5.00 price tag suddenly seemed steep, now that I was unemployed. Nonetheless, the coffee and rich milk calmed my nerves. For the first time, I noticed the soothing spring air and bumble bees floating among the greenery, tending to their buds and blooms. I was breathing. I was OK.

"I really enjoyed my job. Management found out about it and fired me."

cartoonstock.com

My phone buzzed.

"Hi. Do you have a minute?" a voice asked. It was Nick.

"Oh, I have a minute. In fact, I have thousands of minutes right now," I said. We both laughed. Nick was checking in from work to see how I was doing. He claimed to have had a fantastic evening with me. I thought he was trying to be nice, just to make me feel better, which he did.

Later that day, I started telling friends about the latest blowup of my career, the traumatic, ugly truth. But soon realized I would need a short, positive version of the story for acquaintances, prospective employers and the outside world.

Exercises

Step One — Feel the Grief

You've lost your job. It hurts. So, let yourself grieve. Wallow for a day or two. Allow yourself to feel the pain. But make sure it's what coach Alison Cardy calls "Clean Pain" vs. "Dirty Pain." [6]

"Clean Pain" is the first sensation when you stub your toe or cut your finger. "Ouch!" It hurts. Feel it and address it. This is the type of pain you leave behind. You know it will lift. For a headache, you might take an aspirin or close your eyes for a nap. For a twisted ankle, you keep it raised and apply ice. When you've lost your job, treat the emotional pain with compassion and kindness. Indulge yourself. Do you want to see a movie? Sit and do nothing? Drink a bottle of wine? Tend to yourself as though you've experienced the death of someone you know well. Because, in a sense, that's exactly what has happened. You've lost a job and a part of your temporary identity, so honor that. Change that happens fast is always uncomfortable. In this case, change ***hurts***. A lot.

"Dirty Pain," on the other hand, comes with self-punishment. Don't add to the original pain by piling on self-judgement or self-criticism. Feeling the pain of twisting your ankle is fine — blaming yourself for slipping off the curb or being a klutz will only make matters worse. Don't go there.

This is the conversation you should have with yourself:

I got fired. Wow, this sucks. I feel battered and beat up. I'm a little scared. I'm embarrassed. How am I going to survive financially? I don't know exactly, but I'm going to get through this. I'll figure it out. This could be the best thing that's ever happened to me, but I won't be able to see the positives for a while. Just breathe. What do I want to do today?

This is the conversation you're NOT allowed to have with yourself:

I got fired. I should have seen this coming. I'm a failure. My career is never going to recover from this. How could I be so stupid? I should have left that job. Now look at me. This is a disaster.

Whenever you feel the Dirty Pain coming on, give yourself an imaginary shot of painkiller. *Nope! Not going there.* Chase those thoughts out of your brain and go back to the positive track: *I got fired. Wow, this really hurts. I feel beat up. I'm a little scared. I'm embarrassed. I handled myself well. I'm going to get through this. I know this is probably the best thing that's ever happened to me, but I won't be able to see the positives for a while. Breathe in, breathe out.*

The pain comes because you are receiving and processing new information at an uncomfortably rapid pace. You are learning. By definition, this is good. But in the beginning, absorbing all this change and information simply feels awful.

You might look at it this way: You were given a set of keys. One key freed you from the cage that was your job — all the things you didn't like about it. Another key is going to ignite the engine to start you down the road to a whole new set of opportunities, people, and experiences.

Step Two — Write Your Public Story

While you're telling friends and family what happened and letting their love and support salve your wounds, decide on your Public Story.

Your Private Story may include epithets, insults, and appropriate take-downs describing how stupid or evil or incompetent your former bosses were, and how pathetically they acted while firing you, and how they are going to be much worse off than you because of their pea-sized brains.

Your Public Story, alternatively, should be brief, neutral-sounding and end with a positive, forward-looking idea.

"Look, I need honest feedback. Try not to get caught up in whether or not I'll fire you for it later."

cartoonstock.com

Both your Private Story and your Public Story are true. Your Private Story is for yourself and your closest friends. Your Public

Story is for potential employers, people you don't know well, the public in general. Why? Because the version of the truth that is going to get you the next job is not the whole, messy drama. The reality is, in most situations involving people (e.g., marriages, divorces and most relationships) there isn't just one version of the truth, there are several versions, depending on one's perspective. Thus, you are entitled, and highly encouraged, to create a neutral-sounding, positive story for public audiences for the purposes of landing your next gig and staying positive until you do. Think about how you will feel about the situation a year from now, when you're in a great job that pays more, stimulates you, and opens doors to a whole new set of terrific people and experiences. For example:

Leoni

Private Story

Organization X was a mess — a car wreck upside down in a ditch. I worked day and night to repair and get it driving again. Then I asked for a raise. The board fired me. They suck!

Public Story

Organization X asked me to rebuild the organization and its public reputation. We did that fairly quickly, in about 18 months. They treated me well and I'm having a great summer. I'm looking at a few new opportunities. What are you up to?

Jose

Private Story

The job was a nightmare. My supervisor was incredibly demanding and disorganized. I think he's not all there. It was a disaster from the beginning. He basically told me I was fired with a week's notice. I didn't even get to properly train my replacement. It was humiliating.

Public Story

The job turned out to be more administrative than I thought, so my boss Leon and I agreed that the assignment wasn't the right fit for me. Leon is an icon, so it was great to be able to work with him. Now I'd like to get back into policy and communications, which are my true passions. I'm especially interested in Middle East policy.

Kiyomi

Private Story

Well, I worked for an evil witch, basically. She wanted to fire me from the moment I started. I think she was forced to hire me. She tortured me every day she could. I was determined not to let her force me out before I found another job, so I hung on for two years. The bank was a second-tier organization anyway. I'm so relieved to be out of there.

Public Story

I was recruited to lead a new practice in one of the largest banks in the world. The experience was interesting and definitely taught me a lot about finance and leadership. Now I'd like to return to the nonprofit world!

Skyler

Private Story

They created a job for me after I had been a consultant for eight months and eliminated the position four months later. The CEO is incompetent.

The organization is a mess. But now my resume is stained because I was only been there a year. I'm worried. I'm scared.

Public Story

I was hired as a consultant and stayed for a year. I learned a lot about the industry — I loved the manufacturing world and made a ton of friends. Now I'd like to get a permanent position in strategic communications somewhere in the field. I'm looking at several options. My search is going well!

* * *

What's the DNA of the Private Story? It's honest, lets off steam, and tells the truth of the experience for you. Your Private Story invites your friends to commiserate and dump on the idiots who fired you. Your Public Story, by contrast, should be brief, positive, and forward-looking. Your Public Story shouldn't place blame on anyone — not you, not your former employers. Ideally, your Public Story changes the subject to what you want to talk about: what the landscape looks like, the opportunities you're interested in, what your conversation partner is up to and excited about.

Practice your Public Story with friends. Ask them how it sounds. Repeat. Call other friends and practice. Run through your Public Story in your head and in front of the mirror. What you're looking for is a simple paragraph that ends the conversation about how you lost your job and shifts the subject to your future. You don't want to stumble or ramble when you are actively in the market, attracting your next opportunities.

The next stage (in Chapter 4) involves two categories: mind, body, and spirit healing; and practical steps on the path to your next assignment. They are equally important and should be pursued at the same time. The greatest gifts of this experience will emerge from the time you take to heal.

Staging Your Comeback

It's one of the most lonely times of life. Because you lost this huge part of your existence for a moment.

Ankit

At first I was down and depressed. I felt aimless. But after a day or two I felt better for a couple of weeks — I was enjoying the free time. Then I was like, "What am I doing?"

François

Several times now I thought I had done really well in the final interviews and was expecting a job offer. It's been an emotional rollercoaster for almost a year.

Chikwe

Not having a job can be very difficult. All of a sudden, you have neither a schedule nor a professional identity, and you have lots of time on your hands. You're wondering, "When am I going to get a job?" and "Do I have enough money to ride this out?" You may be asking yourself, "What went wrong?" or even, "What's wrong with me? Am I doomed to fail? Am I a failure?" You have more time than ever to obsess over these questions.

Here is the good news: market research suggests that for many corporate employees, losing one's job not only doesn't hurt one's career prospects, but it often leads to higher compensation and greater long-term career success.

Research on the careers of 18,000 corporate executives conducted for *New York Times* bestseller *The CEO Next Door* found that nearly 70 percent of those who had been let go landed in a new job within six months. An additional 24 percent had a new job by the end of one year. More good news from the study: 91 percent of executives who had been fired took a job of similar or greater seniority. In fact, people who reached the corner office as CEO had on average five to seven significant career setbacks on their way to the top.

The research found that the experience of losing a job could even be an *advantage* in getting a new job and in lifting one's career in the long term. In the *Harvard Business Review,* authors Elena Botlho, BJ Wright, and Kim Powell wrote that "33 percent of executives who had been previously fired were recommended for hire — compared to 27 percent of candidates who had never been fired." [7]

Why?

"Experienced hiring managers know that setbacks are inevitable and want to see how individuals have handled failure in the past. The riskiest hires are the ones who are untested by failure. Executives who have faced failure and learned from it can demonstrate resilience, adaptability, and self-awareness prized in leaders," the authors wrote.

In other words, losing one's job and recovering from it can

build leadership skills, the career assets that garner the highest compensation — and elevation to the higher rungs of the professional ladder.

Consider these examples of successful people who were fired:

"Two days before my 50th birthday, I got fired. It was a punch in the stomach," said former Atlanta radio disc jockey Jimmy Baron in *AARP Magazine:*

> *After 23 years on the radio, I was unemployed, had a new baby, and was clueless about what I would do next. My mom said, 'Why don't you get your real estate license?' I said, 'Mom, that's a terrible idea.' I didn't want a real job, and I certainly didn't want to sell anything. But I took an online real estate course, just to get her off my case. Guess what? I didn't hate it. I actually thought it was fascinating. Real estate is about solving problems for people. It's about helping people improve their lives.*

Jimmy Baron went on to become the top real estate agent in a firm with 550 members. "I've never been happier than I am now," he told AARP at age 58. "It turns out Mom was right — as usual," he said. [8]

> *I felt that Salomon Brothers was the place for me. To say I fit in there and loved what I was doing is an understatement. I reveled in it every minute of the day. But the thing is, fifteen years later, they fired me. I was fired around the time the company was sold. They assembled an executive committee of seven people that decided who stayed and who went.*

One of the committee members did not like me — my crime being that I had been the assistant to his nemesis — and he convinced everyone else to vote against me.... I was worried that [my wife] Sue might be ashamed of my new, less visible status and concerned I couldn't support the family.

That was billionaire Michael Bloomberg, on being being fired from Salomon Brothers after a merger!

Megastar Willem Dafoe recently told the story of getting fired on the set of *Heaven's Gate*, his first Hollywood movie. In an interview with *National Public Radio* host Scott Simon, Dafoe said:

We were sitting for eight hours in a lighting setup, and things were very tense because, already, the movie was running way over. And executives were coming and hassling [Director Michael Cimino] to, you know, pick up the pace and not spend so much money and all that. So it was very tense. And we were sitting in the lighting setup, and someone next to me told me a joke, and I laughed out loud. [Cimino] was under a lot of pressure. He turned around and said, 'Willem, step out!' And then once he did that, you know, I think you heard this audible gasping from all my colleagues. And they just said, 'OK, you're finished.' And I said, 'What happened?' They said...'Your character's finished.' [9]

"And that was it, I was fired," Dafoe told *Vanity Fair.* "I don't really count that as my first movie, although, if you look hard enough, you will see me." [10]

"When you went to Baltimore, you went initially to be an anchorwoman," David Rubenstein asked Oprah Winfrey on his eponymous TV show in 2017. And then, it didn't quite work out?"

"Yeah," the megastar answered. "I got fired." Oprah went on to explain how the incident led to her first talk show job, and a historic career. [11]

Clint Eastwood and I got fired exactly the same day [by Universal Studios]. A man stood across from me and he said to Clint, 'You talk too slow and you've got this chip on your tooth which you refuse to get fixed. And your Adam's apple sticks out. It's ridiculous. It's terrible.' So he said, 'I'm sorry, we have to let you go.' I said, 'Excuse me sir, what is it that I did?' And he said, 'You can't act.' [12]

That was iconic actor Burt Reynolds!

It goes without saying that you need to have built a rainy day fund for these inevitable periods (see Chapter 9). The experts say your savings should be enough to support you for six months. With that safety net in place, the hardest part of getting fired, passed over, or laid off is waiting for the next opportunity to snap into place. The uncertainty and fear can be depressing, even crippling. To avoid sinking under the weight, think of this period as an "extended vacation" — a finite amount of time that is precious and in short supply. It's a limited opportunity to explore new things and develop yourself in ways you won't have time to once your next job starts. Another way to approach is this: **How would you use this time if you knew in advance that you were starting a six-month sabbatical and would have a great job at the end of it?** That's how you want to think of this stage.

So, what to do?

The fear, uncertainty, and lack of confidence are creations of your mind. You control your thoughts. Therefore, an important opportunity of this experience is to build your skills in keeping a positive and healthy mindset. Is that possible? Yes. Is it useful? Very.

This "extended vacation" is a temporary break from your routine that is a time of exploration, research, and positioning yourself to attract the many opportunities and inviting experiences the universe has the capacity to provide.

The valuable opportunity in this situation is to build your mental resilience and learn how to position yourself mentally, physically and spiritually to attract the opportunities the universe is creating for you.

While you are applying for jobs and networking (see Chapter 6), take advantage of the time to do things to develop your passions and creative talent. Activities that nourish your soul are an essential part of the healing process, and an invitation to your spirit to produce the green shoots of rebirth.

Some call this, returning to "your own emotional acre," a concept made famous by author Anne Lamott in her *New York Times* bestseller *Bird by Bird:*

> *Every single one of us at birth is given an emotional acre all our own. You get one, your awful Uncle Phil gets one, I get one,*

Tricia Nixon gets one, everyone gets one. As long as you don't hurt anyone, you really get to do with your acre as you please. You can plant fruit trees or flowers or alphabetized rows of vegetables, or nothing at all. If you want your acre to look like a giant garage sale, or an auto-wrecking yard, that's what you get to do with it. There's a fence around your acre, though, with a gate, and if people keep coming onto your land and sliming it or trying to do what they think is right, you get to ask them to leave. And they have to go, because this is your acre. [13]

What does this mean? It means that during this "extended vacation," you have the right — no, you are encouraged — to rediscover the talents and pursue activities that get shoved to the corners of working life, gathering dust and cobwebs. Now is the time to see what's waiting for you — old hobbies, interests and activities that nourish your spirit, give you pleasure, and remind you of things you enjoy and are good at.

Erica Lazaro, a gifted acupuncturist and healer, says that one of the great joys of life is getting to know who you are. Your "extended vacation" is a chance to notice all the beautiful flowers that grow in your garden of talents — on your own emotional acre — once you clear away the brush and let the sun and rain do their magic. Here are some examples of pursuits to nourish you — activities that you can complete for a sense of satisfaction and accomplishment:

- ◊ Walking/Running/Hiking/Bicycling
- ◊ Home improvements
- ◊ Closet cleaning
- ◊ Volunteering/Part-time job
- ◊ Playing a musical instrument

- ◊ Journaling
- ◊ Reading
- ◊ Painting
- ◊ Pick-up basketball
- ◊ Visiting a senior
- ◊ Babysitting a young relative
- ◊ Yoga
- ◊ Streaming free online programs
- ◊ Taking an IT class

Set up a daily structure for yourself. I like to start the day in a coffee shop, absorbing the energy of people around me. Being in the company of people going about their business pulls one out of the isolation that unemployment can create. This energy is contagious.

Start to do little tasks at home — take a sweater to the cleaners, eradicate that pile of junk next to the bookshelf, sort and remove those stacks of papers and books on your desk, pull a few weeds outside. Taking on small, physical projects declutters your environment and provides a sense of accomplishment.

One summer between jobs, I stripped and stained my bedroom floors, a wood bureau, and night table. I gave the bedroom a whole new look, telling friends I was going for a "Restoration Hardware" look on an "Ace Hardware" budget.

And don't forget your physical health. Take walks, sign up for yoga classes regularly if you can, or work out at a gym. If budget is an issue, stick to walking, hiking, and bicycling. These exercises will clear your mind and keep you healthy.

The loss of a job or opportunity is a time to organize your physical environment, take care of your body, and conduct an internal inventory for the future. The more self-aware you are about what you need and want in a job, the better able you will be to land the right kind of opportunity, and the less likely you will be to land in the wrong gig next time.

In *Coach Yourself to a New Career,* author Talane Miedaner provides extensive exercises to help you deconstruct what you personally need out of work. She writes about a CEO who realized that his obsession with being the first one in the office in the morning and the last one to leave was a hidden need "to be the best" covering a vague but persistent discontent with his life despite achieving high levels of financial, professional and social success. "If I had only known that my need to be the best was driving me, I would have got a lot more sleep!" he said. "The central problem with our unmet needs is that they will drive us to engage in all sorts of negative behaviors — overeating, smoking, drinking, gambling, overspending — and we don't even know why we persist in doing it. In fact, you can consciously know you are doing something that you shouldn't be doing (as you stuff that second chocolate doughnut into your mouth) and yet feel compelled to do it anyway. Such is the power of our unmet needs," wrote Mideaner. [14]

When I took the Personal Requirements Quiz in *Coach Yourself to a New Career*, I learned that my emotional needs include feeling useful, appreciated, in control, and to accomplish/achieve. If we can identify and unpack the inner needs that drive us, we can see unconscious behaviors that may be obvious to others, and can be self-defeating (and self-destructive) if we remain blind to them.

I used to become upset with my team for arriving few minutes late to meetings. To me, punctuality is a demonstration of respect for others' time. I felt it was vital to instill in my young colleagues this value. Later, I realized, there was a need buried in my strong feelings to teach "respect," the way I had been taught as a child a generation earlier. Not only did I care about punctuality itself, but I was unconsciously carrying the need to instill the habit in my team to feel "in control." Yikes!

"Brodman, after giving it much thought, I've decided to let you go for no apparent reason."

cartoonstock.com

Identifying my hidden needs allowed me to let go of this unconscious behavior. My team members know I like to start meetings on time and generally arrive punctually. And I find that the minute or two before the stragglers arrive lets me catch up individually with those who are early. Another benefit: being patient instead of a taskmaster on small stuff is a form of flexibility I can give my team. I traded a need to *teach* respect to being respectful myself of my team members, whom, I remind *myself*, are adults with a lot on their plates.

In summary, as you grieve and consider next steps after being fired, take your time. It's a process. Listen to your inner voice. What do you really want? Now is the time to go for it.

How to Stage Your Comeback
1. Mourn, but move on Feeling discouraged is human, says author Angela Duckworth in her bestseller, *Grit.*[15] With time, feeling discouragement should also spark action and build inner strength.
2. Reset expectations After a layoff, consider changing industries. Maybe this is the opportunity you have been waiting for to make a big change.
3. Set "Mini-goals" Break down large and intimidating goals into small, doable steps. That's how major things get done. Make your mini-goals defined, reasonable and reachable.
4. Own mistakes, but see things from a neutral perspective. What was the learning? Let the learning be the focus — not what you think you did wrong.
5. Don't let bitterness drive decisions Observe your emotions. Be alert for any bitterness, hard feelings, hurt, or a desire to prove a point to the people who fired you. Acting out of hurt or resentment is the best way to repeat the errors of the past, and miss opportunities for new directions.

Resumes, References, and Other Stories

WALL STREET HEADHUNTER CPT HAS GONE FROM PREDATOR TO PREY IN JUST SIX SHORT MONTHS

The New York City-based executive search firm — once the seventh-largest in the US and one of the few publicly traded — is expected to file for bankruptcy on Tuesday after it was rocked by allegations of rampant sexual discrimination.

New York Post, 2011

The summer of 2009 marked the depths of the Great Recession. Dawn, a senior associate at a New York consulting firm, was discovered to be in a personal relationship with a senior partner on her team. "If you don't resign, Rahm [the chairman] is going to fire you," the partner told Dawn, matter-of-factly. As the woman in the relationship before the #MeToo era, Dawn was expected to pay with her job. The firm's actions were a clear case of gender discrimination, all too common in the workplace of the time. With the help of an attorney, Dawn threatened legal action, and won a modest settlement a year later. Not long after the settlement, the firm imploded due to rampant sexual harassment and gender discrimination. The sordid details were plastered all over the tabloids.

So how does this drama appear on Dawn's resume? It doesn't. Many of Dawn's accomplishments — along with a few unflattering episodes — do not appear on her resume. That's because, when you are seeking employment, your resume should tell — as succinctly as possible — the most compelling case you can make to be hired for the specific opportunity you seek.

"This job position is very secure. I guarantee you'll never advance or get promoted."

cartoonstock.com

Accomplishments are important. Presenting yourself as a well-rounded individual is good. But your resume should not be a catalogue of your professional history. It is not meant to be a detailed chronology (unlike an academic *curriculum vitae*).

Your resume is a marketing document — the marketing *brochure* of your career. On a resume, like in a love letter or condolence note, not only *which* facts you present but *how* you present them make the difference between your resume landing you the job vs. getting lost in the pile. You're never going to lie, but the way you describe your accomplishments, and the narrative of your career, is your decision. Your goal is to lay out a compelling story.

A resume should not be five pages, unless you are an academic. I recommend one to two pages for junior professionals, three for mid- and senior-level folks. Much more than that looks like you're pompous or inefficient and/or you don't know how to communicate effectively (a key skill for any employee). Good guides are easily found online detailing the nuts and bolts of resume writing. I particularly like George Washington University's free guide from the Trachtenberg School called "Resumes That Get Noticed." indeed.com, LinkedIn, and many other sites offer excellent guidance as well.

But first, there are key things to know about resumes and references which are critical to landing your next job. Most importantly, your resume is a narrative you should edit each and every time you present yourself for a position. In a competitive job market, you should *tailor* your story to fit each opportunity you seek. That may mean tweaking certain words — adding or subtracting certain accomplishments. Remember the phrase, "Dress for the job you want, not the job you have"? The same applies to the resume. Your resume should paint the picture of your *fit* for a specific role. Much of your resume may not change for a specific application, but given how easily you can make changes, it's foolish not to adjust the language and contents for maximum impact — depending on a specific job description or employer.

Think before you write:
1. The Story What is the overall story you want to tell? Engage the reader. What is the "narrative" of your career? The more you see your experiences as part of a continuing, holistic story — a series of experiences that develop knowledge and strengths in a specific direction — the more your resume can tell that story and attract the right audiences.
2. Transferable Skills Your resume needs to grab a reader's attention in six seconds or less. That's about how much time a hiring manager will spend before deciding to read your application further or move on. Most readers (and algorithms) will focus on the top third of the first page. Therefore, a compelling summary/headline or list of your transferable skills at the top of your resume help potential employers quickly see your value.
3. Word choice Technology plays a dominant role in all aspects of work, including the hiring process. The common use of algorithms mean that humans may not see your resume unless it written to pass through computer filters. That means your resume should have words that match up exactly with the language in a job description. Employers and the algorithms they use will scan for these words when reviewing your resume.

If a position description reads:

Identify and analyze federal laws and policies that could impact the viability and success of certain retail financial products. Create processes and procedures to guarantee compliance with relevant laws and regulations. Assess and evaluate relevant global laws and regulatory regimes. Develop and recommend policies and procedures for secure document and records storage in to ensure that the office meets applicable regulatory and oversight body requirements. Outstanding communications skills required.

Your resume should include the following highlighted words:

Identify and ***analyze federal laws*** and ***policies*** that could impact the viability and success of certain ***financial products. Create processes*** and procedures to guarantee ***compliance*** with relevant laws and ***regulations.*** Assess and evaluate relevant ***global*** laws and ***regulatory regimes.*** Develop and recommend ***policies and procedures*** for ***secure document and records storage*** in to ensure that the office meets applicable regulatory and ***oversight*** body ***requirements.*** Outstanding ***communications skills*** required.

Use active verbs. Rather than saying you were "responsible for" a function, use words such as:

- Led
- Managed
- Directed
- Built
- Transformed
- Drove
- Designed

Use words that signal recognition by and positive interaction with others:

- Recruited
- Awarded
- Selected
- Recognized
- Nominated

And: Quantify, quantify, quantify! Listing quantified accomplishments is a shorthand that tells prospective employers, "I am results-oriented and I produce!" without your ever writing or saying so. Find a way to describe your accomplishments with numbers and data!

A few "before and after" samples:

Before: Chief fundraiser for Northeast and Mid-Atlantic Regions, responsible for strategy and execution, including managing 13 development officers.

After: Increased annual giving 27% across major and mid-level gifts in the Northeast and Mid-Atlantic Regions by motivating a team of 13 to exceed goals in nine of the last ten quarters, growing regional portfolios to $4 million, including $2.5 million in gifts from new donors.

If the results of your job are hard to quantify, think of what would happen if you weren't there to do that job. For example, if you are an administrative assistant in the busy development team described above, you can tie your duties to the accomplishments of the team.

Before: Scheduled meetings, sent out invitations, and assisted donor stewardship and prospect engagement efforts for senior leaders of regional development teams.

After: Managed calendars, travel, and administrative operations for 14 development team members who grew revenue 18% from major donor pool of 250, exceeding fundraising goals in nine out of ten quarters.

Also, if you're responsible for sending invitations and communications, you can report on increased volume of communications and open rates. As in: "Increased newsletter open rates from 11% to 26% in first 12 months."

The Resume Checklist
1. Think of your resume as your professional story. Tell it in the most compelling and succinct way possible for the job you want.
2. Avoid job descriptions. Focus on results. Quantify, quantify, quantify!
3. The top third of your resume needs to sell you and your transferable skills in 10 seconds.
4. Use active verbs and words like "recruited" and "awarded" as evidence of recognized accomplishment.
5. Tailor your resume for each position you seek. Use specific words that match the words in the job description.
6. Don't be modest!

Resume and References Case Study: Josh

Josh, a recent graduate with a master's degree in political science from a top university in Washington, D.C., approached me at a career fair where I was speaking. As he shook my hand, I noticed beads of sweat on his forehead. His hand felt cold and clammy. Quietly, he said, "I was laid off from a job after six months. I really think it's preventing me from getting hired again."

I could see the worry on Josh's face. In a follow up note, he wrote:

"Since I was let go roughly a year ago, I feel like there is no good way for a 24-year-old to talk about being fired. I've had about six in-person interviews at a variety of firms (market research, international development, non-profit grant writing, etc.) and no matter how I broach my [Company X] experience...it doesn't work. I've tried to talk about it obliquely, while emphasizing other work roles; I've tried to talk about the learning experience; I've tried to talk about 'my side' and discuss how the environment was hostile and I wasn't a good fit. No matter what, hiring managers see the episode as a huge black mark even though I think the split was relatively amicable and I even got severance pay."

One year later, Josh was convinced that the short episode was preventing him from getting a job in research and policy analysis. Or any job. Period. The truth was, worrying about explaining the abbreviated assignment at Company X was undermining Josh's confidence in every interview and hampering his job search as a whole. Even Josh's resume lacked certainty and punch. This may have been a result of his diminished confidence from his *perception* of the chain of events at Company X.

Josh had an impressive background that included a graduate degree, scholarships, academic honors, awards, published articles, and volunteer experience. He wanted to work for a think tank or policy organization. But the very first lines on his resume, his "Professional Summary," did not express his desires or paint the picture of a dynamic thinker and writer:

> *Professional Summary: Experienced researcher and technical writer with excellent capacity for organizational, administrative,*

and communications workflows as well as policy analysis.

"Capacity for organizational, administrative and communications workflows"? To me, this language sounded like jargon — a string of multi-syllable, technical nouns. Josh had found the phrase online and thought it was generic enough to get him into different kinds of searches. But to me, it lacked a sense of purpose and assets. The phrase was lacking a pulse. Nothing on his resume jumped out and grabbed my attention. I could tell from his emails that Josh was an excellent writer and very smart. Yet, these valuable assets were not coming through in his resume.

We worked together and changed the first lines to:

Objective: Seeking engaging research opportunities in leading organization promoting pragmatic policy reforms domestically and internationally.

This sentence described Josh's interests and his ambition to work for a top organization. Then, I urged Josh to sharpen the descriptions of his prior assignments. More active verbs, more results. At one point, Josh said he was conflicted about being in the job market at all, because he was considering going back to school to earn a Ph.D. This inner conflict was coming through loud and clear in his monotone resume. Josh needed to add color to the story to stand out from the crowd. There was no need to exaggerate, but the resume needed spice. I urged Josh to turn generic terms like "federal agencies" into specifics. Having worked at the "Department of Justice" is more informative and more impressive than for "a federal agency."

After honing Josh's resume, we turned to his worry that a bad reference from an employer who terminated him after six months was killing his job prospects. No matter how the experience ended, nothing is embarrassing about a six-month assignment, I explained to Josh. In the increasingly gig-oriented economy, six months may be a *lengthy* assignment. Josh needed a new description of the episode for his interviews.

"Pardon me — when I suck the enthusiasm out of a new employee too quickly, I get gas!"

Josh believed that the assignment had ended on good terms with the CEO, who promised a positive reference, but the HR chief — the CEO's wife — was giving less than positive references to prospective employers who called. The dynamics Josh described could easily be called "a weird work environment." Put simply, small, family-run businesses can have complex social dynamics that larger organizations don't. When the CEO and the head of HR are spouses, for example, the whole business is their creation. These environments are often intense and difficult to navigate.The fact that Josh lasted six full months in his job and was told he would leave with a positive reference was, in fact, quite an accomplishment.

In interviews, Josh needed to shift from feeling embarrassed about the duration of the assignment to describing his accomplishments in a positive way.

> **Old:** "It wasn't a fit and they fired me after six months. The CEO liked me, but his wife didn't. She was head of HR, and it was kind of weird. "

> **New:** "I worked there six months and learned a good deal about government contracting. The experience sparked my interest in researching and writing about policy, which are my passions."

Josh did not need to go into detail about his original expectations of how long the assignment would be. Better to talk about what he learned in the assignment and skills he strengthened.

"I am worried they are giving me a bad reference."

Josh feared that the HR chief was giving him negative reviews when called by his prospective employers. Therefore, I suggested that he avoid including any references from Company X. Josh had other references he could use.

References should be glowing! Legally, prior employers are prohibited from saying anything more than confirming employment dates, but the truth is, a negative impression can be communicated quite easily.

"Frank?" a prior boss might say, "Yeah, Frank was pretty good." Such a luke-warm reference can easily sink a candidate for a new job.

Your references should have (or have had) an executive title at the organization, but they don't necessarily need to have been your direct supervisor. Find your fans from past organizations and let them do the talking. If you do not expect a good reference from an employer, do not include a representative of the organization in your reference list.

If pressed, you may need to tell a prospective employer why a good reference from a previous employer is not likely. Josh learned that his suspicions were correct — a hiring manager at prospective employer Company Z revealed that Company X's head of HR had indeed given a negative reference.

Josh knew that he had been criticized at Company X for being unresponsive to feedback.

"I tried to preempt the negative reference by acknowledging that I wasn't always good at seeking out ways to improve. When I got the call from Company Z asking to explain the negative reference, I think they found me more credible and sympathetic because I had already acknowledged that this was something I was working on."

The hiring manager at Company Z (and most people) understand that work environments can be complex, and departures can be bumpy. In Josh's case, being prepared with a short, simple explanation and owning his growth areas trumped a bad reference.

That said, it's better to steer a prospective employer to references that will be positive.

Also, if you have a choice between a well-known person in your field who may not have time to give you the full-throated recommendation you seek, versus a less prominent person who will sing your praises to the balconies, definitely choose the latter.

In executive positions, the reference check is usually a victory lap — a *pro forma* exercise to affirm a hiring decision that's already been made. The only major lapse which can sink a candidate at that point is a luke-warm reference. Don't let that happen to you!

It may seem obvious, but always ask your references before providing them to a prospective employer. Most colleagues like to be asked to play this important role as a favor, but not always. If your potential reference hesitates, or you aren't sure he or she can deliver a passionately positive reference, ask someone else.

When you expect your references are going to be contacted by your prospective employer, prepare them. At the very least, alert them to the expected reference inquiry. Be clear about what position you are seeking and how enthusiastic you are about it. Send a brief job description. Then, list a few qualities or accomplishments you would like your reference to highlight. Most references will be grateful for succinct, detailed instructions. Why? Because you're saving the reference time and enabling them to be effective. You want your references to feel your excitement and know how important their support is.

Remember Josh? About a month after our conversations, he messaged me.

"My job search is finally over and in the end I was actually able to pick between two offers! I'll be starting as a consultant working in commercial real estate — not too relevant to the policy space but very interesting with lots of travel. My long-term goal is still to become a professor. My grad school applications are in."

It turned out that making few tweaks to his resume, throwing an old monkey off his back, and sharpening his technique to neutralize a negative reference helped Josh get multiple job offers. A few years later, Josh is a successful nonprofit fundraiser. Finding purpose-driven organizations a better fit than academia, Josh lives happily in Atlanta with his partner and their Plott Hound "Klara."

The Reference Checklist
1. Choose references who will sing your praises enthusiastically and credibly.
2. Don't offer a reference you think will give a luke-warm or negative review.
3. Ask your references for permission before you give their names to a prospective employer. If a reference hesitates, don't risk it. Better not to list them than risk a negative or tepid review. You don't have to tell them if you make that decision and don't list them. Things may change.
4. Prepare your references with a detailed description of the position you seek, the organization, what you want your reference to say about you, and, if possible, a description of the individual who will be calling your reference. At the very least, write an email. Ideally, follow up with a call.
5. If your reference is willing, debrief by phone, text, or email after the reference check. The reference may have gleaned useful information about expectations of the employer, company culture, and even whether there are other candidates seriously under consideration.

6. When leaving a position on good terms, ask for a "To whom it may concern" letter of reference written by your supervisor which you can use in future job applications. You may not ever use the letter, but there is no harm in such a request. Including a glowing reference statement with a future application/cover letter may be a plus.

From Social Media to the C-Suite: Networking On- and Off-line

> Daniel Kim, 22, is finishing his [undergraduate] economics degree at New York University (NYU). After he submitted more than 50 résumés [with no response], he switched tactics and tried to find connections who could make meaningful introductions. Mr. Kim said he recently met an NYU alum who is a dentist, and [also] the wife of a friend of his mother. She offered to connect him with patients who work in finance and he got a meeting, he said. He's now applying to Korean-American banks – hoping he may have an edge for entry-level roles because he speaks Korean – and is considering jobs in real estate. [16]
>
> — ***The Wall Street Journal*, March 2023**

Informational Interviews

A young woman with long, black hair in a pony tail was waiting for me in the reception area of our office. As a favor to an acquaintance in our office building, I had agreed to meet Chanel for an "informational interview" — the term for a meeting requested by a job seeker with an employer with the understanding that the job seeker does not expect to receive a job offer, but would like to learn more about opportunities in the employer's company or field.

My acquaintance in the building didn't even know Chanel well, but since I always tried to honor such requests (which land in my in-box once or twice a week), I agreed. I had scheduled this conversation for a Monday morning 30 minutes ahead of the weekly team meeting in my office to make sure this appointment would be brief. I didn't want to spend too much time at the start of a busy week.

Dressed in a maroon blouse and black slacks, Chanel looked professional and put-together. Her hair was neatly tied back, she was wearing flats and a touch of make-up. Despite feeling a little harried on a Monday morning, as we walked to my office and I offered her coffee, I started to enjoy her presence and the energy and competence she exuded. We sat down. Chanel thanked me for my time repeatedly as she started to explain her passions, her past jobs, and plans for her career.

Within a minute I started to think that Chanel was a perfect candidate for an open, entry-level position on our fundraising team. She had worked with movie directors and producers at Creative Artists Agency, the top Hollywood talent firm, and in the promotions department at Universal Pictures. She left Hollywood to find work that aligned with her passions for helping women in the developing world. On the side, she had started her own social enterprise to help young women in Africa. I could see Chanel was a polished communicator, able to handle stressful situations and big egos, and entrepreneurial. She had demonstrated that she was a self-starter for asking for this meeting and following up until we could arrange a suitable time (including a few delayed responses by me).

Whirling her rose-tinted MacBook open during our meeting, Chanel sent me her resume instantly when I asked for it as she was sitting in my office and my team filed in. Chanel had already said yes to another job, but I knew we had a better opportunity for her that would match her passions and allow her to grow. As my teammates sat down next to Chanel on a soft, white IKEA sofa with batik pillows, I could see they liked her immediately, too. Somewhat to the surprise of all of us, I offered Chanel the fundraising job on the spot. Chanel informed the other company that she would decline their offer and accepted ours.

Weeks later, our Human Resources department had gathered a dozen resumes which had been submitted online in application for the same position. None of candidates were anywhere near as impressive and right for the job as Chanel. Hiring Chanel saved us weeks or months of precious time and earned kudos from our CEO for bringing in such a great addition to the team.

Hiring Chanel on the spot might have been unusual, but the vast majority of jobs are indeed filled through referrals, recommendations, and *coincidences.* That is, a hiring manager asks her network for help in filling a position, and somebody recommended through the network usually gets the job. Timing matters.

It was "lucky" for Chanel and for us that she came in for an "informational interview" which turned into a successful job interview for an open position. As "luck" would have it, Chanel's informational interview had been postponed a few times to a date that was perfect in terms of our hiring schedule. However, Chanel's "luck" was a result of her smart and persistent networking. In this case, Chanel had asked her boyfriend's friend, someone who worked at another firm in our building, to make an introduction to people in his network who might be able to help her access resources and opportunities in the nonprofit world. Draper asked me if I would meet Chanel. Because I like Draper, and I generally try to say yes to such requests, I agreed. Chanel had to follow up a few times in emails with me to make the meeting happen, as my schedule can be tight. But she did. Chanel turned out to be a superstar on our team. Hiring her was one of the best decisions of my career.

A critical step in building a career is expanding your networks so that you will be in the right place at the right time when opportunities open. "Luck" happens a lot more when you are connected to the networks through which continuous informal recruiting efforts flow.

Effective Networking

In my career, literally nine out of ten jobs I landed were the result of a recommendation by someone I knew. Dawn Graham writes in her book *Switchers* that more than 70 percent of jobs are filled through networking. Says Graham:

> *Think about how you hire when you have an open position. Is your first step to pay large sums of money to post the role on big job sites? Probably not. First, you likely think about people you have worked with previously. Many jobs are filled by managers bringing in their former team members. Then, you inquire with your network. Is there anyone your trusted contacts might recommend for the role? Guess what? The companies you're applying to are taking this approach, too. If networking fails to produce a candidate, they'll next post the position internally, so only current employees in the organization have access to it. If there are still no bites, the role will be posted on the company's public website (which is free and tends to attract applicants who have a direct interest in the*

organization), and then finally on the mega-job sites. So, how many of the most interesting, highest-paid, sought-after roles do you think make it to the mega-job sites? Awesome jobs are usually filled before the previous employee's chair is cold, so they're rarely advertised. [17]

When there is an open position on my team, not only do I let my networks know about it, but I ask someone on my team to find great candidates on LinkedIn so we can actively contact and potentially recruit them. LinkedIn provides an outstanding platform for recruiting through personal and professional networks.

Therefore, online and offline networking are essential to landing future jobs. And it will make you more successful at any job you have. Knowing whom to call for something is a huge asset in doing your job as well as seeking a new one.

The double-hitter of a strong resume with a recommendation by a trusted source is hard to beat. And when senior leaders ask their networks for recommendations, they often find excellent candidates. Thus, the practice dominates.

But what exactly *is* networking? More importantly, what is *effective* networking?

The purpose of networking for career advancement is to establish a link to people who have access to information or other resources you need to advance your professional goals. More than that, networking is also developing relationships with the people around you — in your field and elsewhere. In our hyper-connected world, it can simply mean sending an invitation to someone on LinkedIn after meeting. Or exchanging business cards. You don't know how or when the contact might be useful to yourself or others down the road.

Some people think networking is a self-centered career advancement strategy. But done right, networking means helping others find the opportunities they seek, as well. Networking includes getting to know the landscape of people who surround you, whether it's the baristas in your Starbucks, or Maybel at the reception desk in the building, or Jorge, the head of the accounting firm in the building who tells jokes in the elevator. All your colleagues and contacts are important people in your landscape.

You should not wait until you're looking for a job to build your network. As a vital aspect of building your career, networking should be a regular — if not daily — practice.

Washington, D.C., headhunter Sherry Ettleson says, "Especially if you're seeking a senior role, it's not about applying online. The key is getting your resume to the right people." Ettleson started executive search by doing a favor for a colleague. She explains, "I was out of work, and a former colleague called me to help him with a search. I said, 'Bill, no one is going to return my calls.' But they did, because they know me, they know I'm a nice person, and they know I'm connected."

Be methodic, advises Ettleson. "I always encourage people to stay organized with their networking," she says. "You have to put it into your schedule. I don't care if it's one hour a week, or ten, but it's got to be part of your schedule. You have to ping people. You have to be strategic. Sometimes you need talking points to make sure you communicate clearly. You need to network as part of your job." Ettleson blocks Friday mornings to speak with job seekers who have asked to meet her. While these meetings are not necessarily relevant to her current search assignments, it's a form of networking that is helpful to those who requested her advice. "You put a favor in the favor bank, and you can take it out again," Ettleson says.

The higher up the career ladder you rise, the more important your network becomes. Why? Not only is your network the key to finding future jobs, but a large network is considered an asset to an acquiring employer. "It's the perception that you know people," Ettleson says. Knowing a wide circle of people helps you do your job. How? You can access advice, resources, and opportunities that otherwise would be out of reach. For senior executives, a strong network is not only valuable, but essential.

"OK, I believe you," you're saying. "But *how* should I network?"

In-Person Networking

Every place you go is an opportunity to meet new people, but when it pertains to your career, the most valuable networking situations involve people related to your field and interests. Professional association events, conferences, gatherings sponsored by vendors like law firms or marketing companies to promote visibility, and networking groups are all good venues for making connections. The holiday party season can be especially rich.

Remember, networking is all about relationship building. Keep your exchanges fun, light and informal — you don't need to talk about your career (much less promote yourself) within minutes of meeting a person. The idea is to get a conversation started. People are more apt to hire, do business, and partner with people they like.

"I'm inviting you to my seminar on Improving Your Communication Skills. If you'd like to attend, grunt once for yes or twice for no."

Be curious, ask questions, and acknowledge the pleasure and value of hearing the thoughts of a new contact. Each person you meet knows something about a topic that might interest you, and you want their perspective and opinions to build your understanding. Listening attentively makes you a good conversation partner, no matter what the context. Even though you might be curious about other potential contacts in the room, do NOT look over someone's shoulder while they're answering your question. Courtesy is paramount. Active listening is a powerful skill to practice at networking events (and in life!).

There is a benefit in attending large events — you can meet a lot of people. Dawn Graham, host of "Dr. Dawn on Careers" on SiriusXM, has developed several strategies for networking in large groups in *Switchers.* She writes: "It's easy to find a reason to skip a networking event ('traffic is ridiculous, I have laundry to do'). I seem to find critical things to do when I'm supposed to be attending a big social event." She suggests inviting a friend or colleague she calls "a wingman." "Having a wingman can help to get to the event, which is half the battle. Just be sure to split up and meet new people instead of solely chatting with one another. You can share your new connections to double the return." [18]

But what if you can't find a wingman or networking buddies? You still need to put yourself out there.

Since networking is such an important part of work, and the key to expanding one's horizons, I use several tricks to push myself to go to evening events when I don't feel like it:

1. Keep it brief

I tell myself, I'm going to stay an hour at most. Or, *I'm going to make it home in time to watch the evening news.* Sometimes good conversations will keep me out longer. But after a long day at work, when I want to go home and relax, I can get myself to a networking event by promising to make it quick.

2. Arrive early

The beginning of a reception — even a few minutes before it starts — is a great time to meet the principals. In the quiet time before the crowds arrive, you can have a real conversation, maybe two or three. Also, at the start of an event, the principals are often standing around anxiously looking for something to do before the crowds arrive. By coming early, you help put their minds at ease during normal pre-party jitters.

3. Look good

The football and baseball star Deion Sanders, who is now a sports announcer, was said to have a philosophy about how his off-the-field wardrobe helped his career. When asked, "Why do you wear all those gold chains around your neck?" Sanders, sometimes called "Neon Deion," reportedly said: "Why do I wear all these gold chains? Because when I look good, I feel good. And when I feel good, I play good. And when I play good, I get paid good!"

His philosophy is useful for those of us actively looking for a job or just keeping an eye on the horizon. Bottom line: Wear clothing that is professional and makes you feel good about yourself.

4. Set the goal of meeting a few new people

Make it a point to introduce yourself to a few new people. This is much easier than it sounds. All you have to do is approach someone and say, "Hi, I'm Barb Sanchez." About 99 percent of the time the person will be flattered by your interest and return your greeting.

5. Conversation starters

Start a conversation with a compliment, like "I love your shoes," or, "Those are cool glasses!" Positive comments put people at ease and make them feel noticed. Remember, at a typical networking event, most people in the room are a little nervous, are among many people they don't know, and are eager meet new people. You're doing them a favor by introducing yourself, even if you feel nervous.

If people are wearing nametags, starting conversations is even easier, such as asking about their organization if it's listed. "What is Dine Brands?" you might ask. "What do you do at PwC?" Then just listen. "What brings you to this event?" is another good conversation

starter or extender. You can learn a lot about organizations and who works at them through these conversations. If someone is wearing a flag pin or button with a message (e.g. "Marine Corps Veteran"), ask about it.

Chatting about mutual friends and acquaintances can also a useful topic. A person may reference an organization where you have a contact. "Do you know Samia Smith? I think she works in government affairs at X." Often the answer is yes, leading to a conversation about mutual friends and colleagues. The "do you know..." conversation is not only fun, but lets people in a conversation talk more about themselves and their acquaintances. So it has the triple benefit of being an enjoyable conversation while also bringing out professional history and identifying mutual contacts.

Some research says that half of the people at networking events find it challenging, so look for people standing on their own. Most will be glad if you approach them and introduce yourself. If you see folks wandering the floor without a group, reach out your hand and invite them to join yours. Networking does not mean only speaking to the extroverts in the room.

6. Get personal

Sometimes, I like to ask people where they're from, or where they live, as an ice breaker. It makes the conversation more interesting and gets people away from canned "elevator speeches." Ultimately, the goal of networking is to connect with people. Ask people what their commute is like. This conversation almost always leads to the result of exchanging cards and establishing a connection — people love to commiserate about traffic and weather!

7. Set reasonable goals

If you have met three people and want to go home, go! Networking should be a regular practice, not an exhausting enterprise. Keep it fun and sustainable — and accommodate your desire to relax at home and get your rest.

8. Business cards — A must!

Do you have a business card? If you are between jobs, get one. Business cards may seem old fashioned, but they're professional and practical. I recommend cards that have an identity beyond your address and phone number. Sonia was looking for a job in international development in Washington, D.C., and had done some consulting while job hunting. She didn't have a company or a website, but that's not necessary for establishing a "shingle" for the purpose of business cards. Examples:

Sonia Gandhi
Global Advisory Partners
Contact information (including your X handle/website if applicable)

or

Beri Mitchum
Writer-Researcher-Policy Analyst

Bridget Yoo
Strategic Communications Advisor

Antonio Bejar
Marketing Strategist

Business Cards by Sneh on
www.fiverr.com/sneh

A freelance TV producer I know also adds her photo to the card, so that people remember what she looks like. Her card stands out. She said the image helps people remember her when they're sifting through their stack of newly acquired business cards from a conference. Use both sides of the card!

You don't need the fanciest business cards, but find something attractive and high quality online. Carry LOTS of them and hand them out. Each time you do, you're taking a powerful step in your networking. The card is a tool that employed people use — conveying that you are *in the workplace,* not stuck outside. Your business card lets people find you again in a few months if they can't remember your name but want to contact you.

If a networking conversation is going well, I often say, "Let me give you my card." The suggestion is courtesy and a sign of respect, a typical interaction between employed people. People usually respond, "Yes, let me give you mine" or "I've run out, but I'll email you."

Sometimes, I'll ask, "Do you have a card?" The question is a tacit acknowledgement that you find the person desirable to know. If a person doesn't have a card, an apology and a promise to email usually follows. These days, finding people on LinkedIn is so easy, you can send an invitation to connect regardless. With or without business cards, exchange contact information.

9. Making an exit

Leaving an event sometimes involves extricating yourself from conversations. Doing this gracefully is a good skill.

Examples:

"I hate to leave, but I have an early flight tomorrow."

"I still have some work to do tonight so I need to scoot. It was so nice to meet you!"

"It's been great talking with you. I need to get home to walk my dog. I hope we can stay in touch!"

Always be sure to thank the event hosts before you leave. (Search for your hosts if necessary!) Hosting events is a lot of work, and it's a very nice gesture to thank (and compliment) the hosts and their staff. Not only is it polite and kind, but it's a good way to be invited again.

10. What should I say about my job search?

If you're unemployed, say you are "exploring next steps" in your career or "interviewing for a new position." The premise for a conversation about your job search should be framed as "asking for counsel," "picking your brain," or "getting a sense of the landscape" in a particular field.

When new contacts agree to talk in person about your search, forget about asking for a job. Think of your exchange as doing research and possibly building a new relationship that might be mutually beneficial in the future. If the conversation goes well, ask whether your new contact might be open to an "informational interview."

What not to say: I've been looking for a job for 10 months. I'm miserable.

What not to say: Are you hiring?

What to say (A): "I've always respected your company and know of your excellent reputation. You must be very busy, but it would mean so much to me to be able to pick your brain for a few minutes about the landscape as I explore next steps in my job search — if you have time."

What to say (B): "I have always been impressed with [your organization's] work. Since moving here last month, I'm exploring opportunities in the humanitarian sector and would be so grateful for an informational interview, if you have time."

Try to get an in-person meeting, but definitely take a call or Zoom if the person suggests it rather than a meeting. Sometimes, a good call will lead to a meeting, but the bottom line is to be respectful of the contact's time. And remember, networking is a two-way street — building this relationship means you may be in a position to help this contact in the future. You never know.

And don't forget to say "yes" when people you don't know ask for *your* time and help. Pay it forward!

11. The follow-up note

Should you send a follow up note? Yes, if you would like to stay in touch with your new contact. Send a short email or text. Keep it friendly, professional and respectful. A follow-up note can simply convey that you enjoyed meeting the person and look forward to staying in touch. If you discussed a follow-up meeting, you should include your desire to schedule it. Include your contact information! In most circumstances, I simply send a LinkedIn invitation as a follow up, sometimes with a message to remind the person that we met. Example:

Dear Jaime,

It was great to meet you at the WNG happy hour. Who knew WNG would serve up such excellent sushi? We don't have to go to Tokyo! I would love to hear more about your work and pick your brain about my next steps. Might you have time for coffee near your office? I would be grateful for a few minutes.

Many thanks,

Beth

Beth Solomon
202-222-2222
bethsolomon1@gmail.com

The In-Person Meeting

Meeting people at events is critical to expanding your networks and positioning you for future opportunities. But it often takes an in-person (or Zoom) meeting or phone call to talk in-depth about specific opportunities and start to establish a professional relationship. In a world increasingly dominated by technology, the power of a personal connection — even having met once — becomes more significant. Make your requests as personal as possible to convey the depth of your interest. For example:

"What a pleasure to meet you at the SFIG reception last month. I really appreciated your tips on installing solar panels. In fact, we're talking with two separate vendors now about following your lead! My niece is graduating from Michigan this spring, and I'm trying to help her learn more about opportunities in the hotel business. Is there any chance you might talk with her for 15 minutes via Zoom or FaceTime? I would be so grateful."

One-to-one conversations are also a great way to learn whether certain fields or organizations might be a good fit — and just as importantly — whether they might not.

Be sure to convey that you are seeking information and perspective, not a job. Asking for an "informational interview" is a handy shortcut to convey your intent, making it clear you are not requesting to be hired as a result of the meeting.

When asking for a meeting with someone I don't know, I like to reference the person's reputation as a leader or expert or someone who is knowledgeable in their field, and express how much I would appreciate the benefit of their perspective. Consider the phrase, "I would be grateful for your advice." Or "I would like to run a few ideas by you." The latter phrase indicates that you have ideas to share and are not expecting the conversation to be a one-way extraction of information.

Compliments are surprisingly helpful. As mighty and self-confident as some people might appear, even those in high places have insecurities and need positive reinforcement. If you admire a leader you hope to talk with, let them know how much you respect them. I like the words, "You are a great role model." Such words enhance your requests for a busy person's time.

Think of each person you meet as important to your network. They are flowers in a garden you are growing. Relationships you want to cultivate. When you meet contacts, and when you communicate with them later, don't hesitate to ask if you can be of help in any way. Find ways to be useful, like following their LinkedIn profiles and liking their posts. Compliment them for being quoted in an article or for writing a good blogpost.

Social media opens up whole new solar systems for networking online...

Online Networking / Social Media

Online, you need to make your professional brand known to a broad audience: people you know, people you don't know — and headhunters. When someone googles you, your LinkedIn profile often shows up at the top of the search results. Increasingly, headhunters use LinkedIn as their primary source of candidates. So developing your profile is worth time and effort. Personal branding expert, William Arruda of *Forbes,* says there are several characteristics of a compelling LinkedIn profile, including completeness, consistency, and keeping your profile up-to-date.[19] The following characteristics, in my view, are the most important elements to consider:

1. **Potency.** When someone looks at your profile, they are only provided with a brief glimpse into the full content of your career. The initial snapshot must compel them to click further. Use short, punchy, active language whenever possible.

2. **Visual appeal.** LinkedIn's research shows that posting a photo makes your profile 14 times more likely to be viewed by others. 14 times! If you already have a recent headshot taken by a professional photographer or have the opportunity to get one, this is a good investment. A photographer can ensure that the lighting is flattering, the context is right, and the size and resolution of the photos are professional quality. A professional photo can cost $200 to $500, well worth the cost. A good photo is much more visible than say, a new suit. If you don't have the budget, ask a friend to be your photographer.

3. **Activity**. LinkedIn has been adding features to allow you to post multimedia content to your profile like photos, media clips, and videos. Use them to your advantage:

- Choose a good background photo. This photo sits behind your picture and is one of the first things people see in your profile. Replace the generic background with a photo or graphic that illustrates what you do or what you would *like* to do. On the internet, visuals are usually more powerful than words alone.
- Write posts and articles. Writing about events and achievements draws attention to your profile, even if they have nothing to do with your job.

4. **Personality.** Headhunters, potential employers, and contacts want to see your credentials and experience, but they are ultimately humans attracted by human qualities. Expressing your personality in the way you write your summary and describe your experiences is vital. Add content that goes beyond your accomplishments and credentials. Give your profile flavor by including your passions and interests in posts and photos. Ask friends to look at your profile and provide feedback.

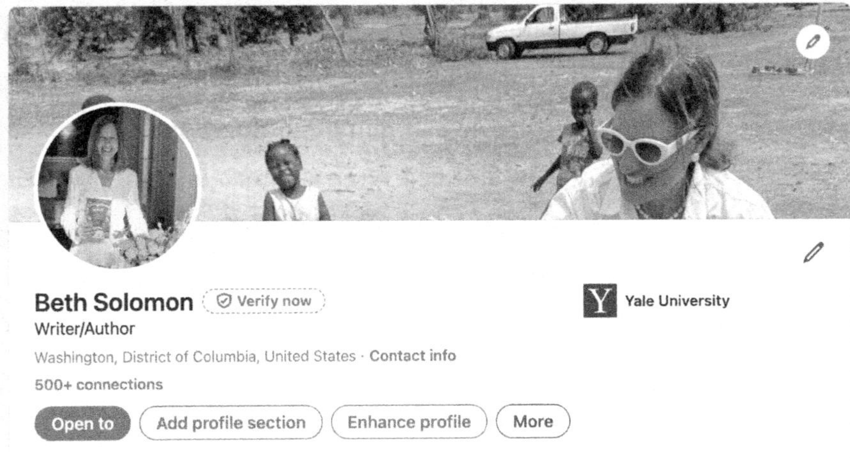

With over half a billion members and a focus on professionals, LinkedIn is not only essential in job searching, but full of potential as a career builder.

In large part due to LinkedIn, I receive many requests to talk with people about career transitions they want to make. This has been true for years. When I ask people why they wanted to talk with me, the answers are usually a combination of, *You seem successful, You have done a lot of different things* and *You know a lot of people.* What they're seeing is the brand I have created for myself online, especially on LinkedIn. For a long time I have used these platforms to share moments and experiences when I am having the most fun at work. Instead of posting about office life, I usually post pictures from professional events and link to people who were there. Sharing these moments is not only enjoyable, but practical. Posting makes me visible to my network of contacts, and beyond.

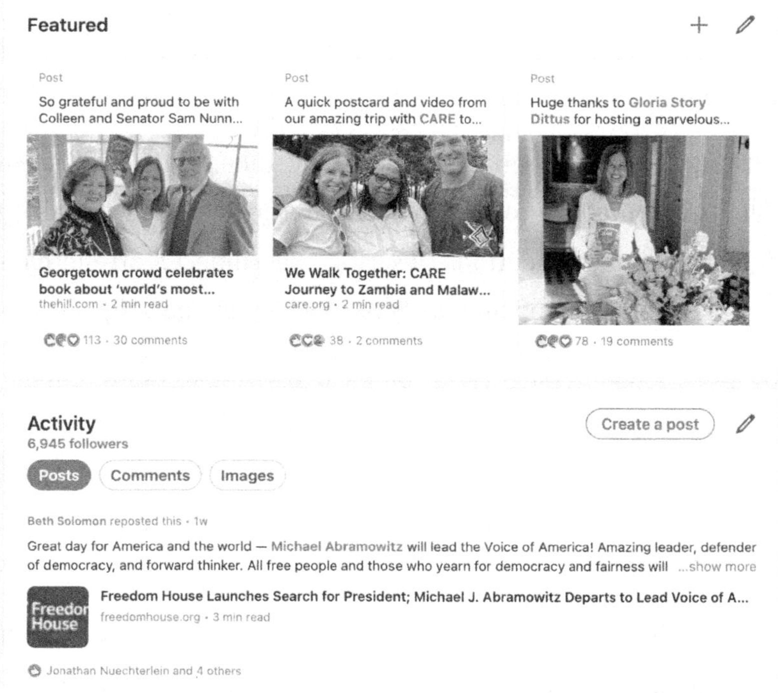

Leveraging LinkedIn

You can get started right away on LinkedIn. Each day, post a few comments and "like" the posts of some of your online contacts. Pass along a job opening to former colleagues who might find it interesting. And endorse the skills of people you know on LinkedIn. People who use LinkedIn get a message when you take the simple step of endorsing skills like "leadership," "communications," or even "Microsoft Word." Endorsing someone's skills is like sending a little gift. It's a public compliment that enhances a person's online profile. And it's easy and free!

When you are so inclined, write "recommendations" on LinkedIn. "A recommendation is a statement that is written by a LinkedIn member to recognize or commend a connection, such as a colleague, business partner, or student. People who view your profile will often read the recommendations you've received from your connections to see what others have to say about your work," according to LinkedIn.

Writing a recommendation need only take five minutes. First, get the attention of the reader. Make a reference to your authority in making the recommendation. Describe the subject's strengths and value with a personal touch. And make your language sing:

"Cindy Grande is one of the smartest and most talented financial executives I have ever worked with. At Bank X, her understanding of the market and ability to handle multiple projects dramatically increased the productivity level of our company. On top of that, she is a fantastic person!"

You will be amazed at how grateful people are when you write LinkedIn recommendations for them. Those who are active online want people to "see" them. You can offer encouragement, support, and enthusiasm — acknowledgements we all crave in our professional lives. Think of this form of networking as a way to help others rather than yourself. You will experience the rewards almost immediately.

Your LinkedIn presence is your most public professional presentation of yourself. Put some time and energy into making it sparkle.

"Good afternoon, Ted, I'm your online presence."

cartoonstock.com

Online Networking Checklist
1. Take time each day to network on LinkedIn.
2. Make sure your online profile is professional, personal, and potent.
3. Post a professional-looking headshot.
4. Endorse the skills of colleagues, post articles and photos, send messages, and write recommendations.
5. Don't wait until you are looking for a job to engage with this powerful networking tool.

A Note about Virtual Networking

The pandemic made networking extremely challenging.

"Getting *any* time with people was really really difficult," said Victoria, who was laid off during Covid in Boulder, Colorado. "So many people were overwhelmed, they didn't have time to network. A kid got sick, somebody else got sick. People were already super busy, and finding time for regular networking was an added layer. And then it was all through zoom. People got so zoomed out that the time or the attention people had was gone." Victoria contacted an old friend for a networking Zoom call, for example, but the Zoom was rescheduled six times. "By the time we talked the energy had left the situation," Victoria said. "People would say, 'Yeah, good luck with your search.' They were beyond strapped."

In-person networking is back, according to Sherry Ettleson, but after working from home for two or three years, building back in-person meeting and socializing skills will take effort. For young people who have worked remotely more than in-person, the current situation poses challenges.

"Networking has definitely changed since COVID," said Imani, a twenty-eight-year-old marketing manager in San Francisco. "I'm fully remote now. We used to be in WeWork. That was such a good way to meet people. We ended up meeting in the kitchen making food at the same time or getting beers together — it just happened spontaneously. Now I'm just looking for jobs and trying to connect on LinkedIn. I've gotten used to it now, but I definitely miss that in-person element. My team has some in-person meetings, but there's just not that much opportunity to meet people from other companies. I'm reaching out to people I don't know or reaching out to someone I know and asking them if their company might have jobs in marketing. It's tough. It definitely is," Imani said.

The COVID-19 pandemic clearly made networking a bigger challenge. However, working remotely makes networking even more necessary. Basically, you need to meet new people, activate your old network, and get your resume seen by folks who might be leads to your next job.

Reach out to former colleagues, old friends, folks you haven't spoken within a while. While the absence of live events during COVID was challenging, the upside is that people are starved for human contact and connection. Make phone and Zoom appointments. Ask people to look at your resume. Sign up for virtual events. The key to virtual networking is the same as live networking — you want to meet new people as longterm friends and partners in your career, not just as sources for jobs.

Example: Machelle was looking for a job in communications. Her former colleague at a business newspaper moved to a role in communications at a large global bank. Machelle spoke with him as she started her job search, looking for communications consulting work, but six months later, she revised her resume and was looking for a permanent job. Jon, the former colleague, had been generous with his time and counsel the first time. Machelle wondered whether he would think her a nuisance for calling again. Rather than ask about opportunities at the bank, Machelle asked Jon if he would look at her new resume and give her some counsel on the changed job landscape since the first time they spoke. Jon was happy to help her.

Machelle paid a coach to help her rewrite her resume and make a few introductions in the city where she wanted to work. Then, she landed a job at a top public affairs firm in Washington — negotiating a partially remote arrangement — within a year of starting her search.

Networking is an essential practice in building a successful career. Make it regular, make sure to pay it forward, and make it enjoyable. In addition to participating in large, organized events, how about asking five present and former colleagues to each bring a friend to a bar or cafe for a happy hour next week? Networking doesn't have to be complicated. Make it fun!

The Interview

After they told me I was laid off and would only receive one more week of pay, the whole next 48 hours was existential dread. I have five kids — you could even say six because I pay child support to my ex-wife. So my salary literally pays to keep the lights on.

Luckily, my first interview came fast. A prominent think tank called in response to my online application. I was so tense because it felt like life or death to get this job. The interview took place three days after I got whacked. It happened very fast, which was good. But I was not in a good place. When I get stressed, I start talking too much and too long.

The conversation was going fine, and then the hiring manager asked a standard interview question, 'What's your greatest weakness?' I was too honest. I said, 'I'm not organized enough.' And then I started saying I had this deputy in a former job, who was amazingly organized, and we were a great team because she was the organizer and I was the visionary. And then I said, 'On the other hand, I think I may undersell myself because I actually think I am better organized than many people.' And I just started waxing on about the concept of being organized.

As I was talking, I was thinking to myself, WHAT AM I DOING??? I was going down a rabbit hole because I was so panicked. I never heard back from the think tank. I could tell I had blown it.

The good news is that I immediately knew what was wrong and vowed to do better. I hadn't interviewed in a long time and that was my first one. After that interview, I started writing down what I was going to say to some of those standard questions. I realized I needed to be more prepared; I couldn't wing it. So I remember, the next interview — it might have been for the job I got — I nailed it. I decided, if someone asks me about my weaknesses, what am I going to say? Whatever I said, it was like two sentences and then I shut up.

I'll never forget it when, after I had met with several members of the team at a respected organization about three weeks later, the hiring manager said, 'What do we have to do to attract you?' A wave of relief passed through me.

CARLOS, MEDIA RELATIONS EXECUTIVE

Congratulations! You've made it to the job interview. This is the most intense and exciting moment in a job search — usually a live, spontaneous performance involving at least two actors, the hiring manager and you. Usually, you will have several in-person or Zoom meetings with other members of an organization before getting hired.

The hiring manager's job in the interview is to "sell" the job opportunity to you while subtly probing for any weaknesses or red flags — without being obvious about the latter. Your goal is to be "you" and deliver a performance that leads to a job offer — to come across as qualified, competent, likable, professional. You should also have one eye on potential negatives, watching for warning signs of unappealing aspects of the potential job, including personality characteristics, the nature of the work, evidence of dysfunction, toxic stress, etc. You want to be alert to the subtle elements that create the "atmosphere" in a workplace.

"We're looking for someone who isn't afraid to fire people. You may be overqualified."

©Glasbergen

Usually following an organization's determination that a candidate is qualified for a position, the interview process is to test for personality alignment — whether a candidate is a "good fit." Normally, an organization will phone-screen six to 10 candidates and interview at least three or four of the "most qualified" before making a decision. Often, the final two candidates meet a number of members of the organization. The candidate considered the "best fit" gets the first job offer. Therefore, the interview process, often involving several interviews, is the high stakes final round (not including references, which are often *pro forma* — see Chapter 5) of the hiring process.

Interviewing is nerve-wracking, but should also be exciting. You're meeting new people; you're checking things out. Think of the interview as a performance you can rehearse for — your opportunity to shine. Lights, camera, action!

By all means request in-person interviews rather than Zoom meetings if you have a choice. Going into a job interview in an organization's offices is like visiting someone's house. To begin with, there is so much to learn by sitting in the lobby and watching. Observe the receptionist (if there is a receptionist). Does the person seem content, competent, friendly, solicitous, bored? He or she is part of the ecosystem you are studying. Watch and listen closely.

Next, whether interviews take place in conference rooms or in individual offices, each room tells a story. Notice how coffee, tea, water etc. are offered, the demeanor of administrative staff — all of these are clues to the personality and culture of the organization. Pay attention, because these clues may tell a different story than the image the organization wants to project.

Some things to look for:

1. The receptionist — is he or she friendly, stressed? Rude?
2. Casual interactions — do people treat one another kindly?
3. What is the energy level? Is there energy in the room? Does it feel sleepy? Quiet? Loud?
4. Do people smile? Do you hear any laughter? (Laughing is allowed in the office!)
5. Are there a diversity of ages, ethnicities, and genders?
6. What is the dress code?
7. Is the office up-to-date? Comfortable?
8. Is it an open-concept office, are individual offices occupied? Is the lighting good? Are there windows? Plants?
9. Imagine: how would it feel to work in this place?

The reason to tune into these aspects is that, like visiting someone's house, there are lots of clues about the people, the culture, and working in this setting hiding in plain sight. Think of a job interview not only as a performance, but as an investigative assignment. While your goal may be to land a job offer, you also want to be looking for clues as to whether the organization, the people, and the workplace feel like a good fit for you.

True story: I was pinching myself as I drove through the gates of an iconic Hollywood studio lot for my second interview with a famous movie producer — let's call her "Gail Levy" — whose blockbuster *rom-coms* and dramas featured stars like Matthew McConaughey, Kate Hudson, and Danny DeVito. Pastel stucco walls punctuated by palm trees concealed a world of stars, movie sets, and sound studios on the 65-acre lot in downtown LA. Gail's office was nested in a real log cabin on the lot, hauled from an old ranch in West Texas. Giant leather chairs and rough wooden tree stumps, along with cattle skulls and the Texas flag, decorated the dark, atmospheric cottage. Gail had a lifelong love affair with Texas; her offices made you feel like you were on a ranch somewhere on the sandy, hot plains.

She was looking for an Assistant Producer, someone who would keep track of all the details that go into the actual production of a movie — from ensuring that the blue paint on a wall was the "right" color to managing the shooting schedule, to scheduling Gail's many flights, hotels, and drivers.

After the first meeting in the lodge on the Hollywood lot, a cool, dark shelter under the blazing LA sun, I was thrilled to be considered for the assignment. At the time, life involved sitting behind a desk at a large Hollywood talent agency wearing a headset from eight o'clock in the morning to eight o'clock at night five days a week. My job involved listening to and taking notes on my boss's client calls, scheduling talent meetings with studios, ordering scripts from the in-house copy center, and shepherding minor contracts through the signature process. When the firm closed in the evenings, we would jump in our cars to deliver scripts to the mansions of actors and directors in Benedict Canyon, Malibu, the Hollywood Hills — wherever our clients lived. Talent agencies are the nerve centers of Hollywood — where writers and scripts are connected to actors and directors, where film and TV projects are put together. My job paid minimum wage and was grueling, but was one of the hardest to snag in Hollywood because of the opportunity to learn the industry fast and move up.

The coveted escape route out of these high-end Hollywood sweatshops was, ideally, landing a job as a production assistant at a studio or with a producer. The opportunity to be *Gail Levy's* Assistant Producer would be an unusually high-level jump — like landing a spot as network news reporter as your first job after college.

Our initial interview had gone very well. Gail was smart, charming, funny, and warm, a petite blond with a hearty laugh whose personality filled the room. We talked a little about the job, her background, my background. This was the "seduction" phase of the interview process, which happens when an employer has preliminarily qualified the candidate based on her resume. I briefly met the other two members of the team, administrative assistants who seemed a little reticent, but I was thrilled to be considered and focused on winning over Gail.

Gail told me she was delighted with our first conversation and highly impressed with my credentials and education. After we sailed happily through the initial interview, she asked me to come back for a second round.

A week later I perched on the edge of one of the giant leather sofas on the sheep skins covering the cottage floor. Gail was wearing jeans and had her cowboy boot heels resting atop a vintage steamer trunk. She was a tiny thing, and intense, with the wiring of the transplanted New Yorker she was. No amount of softly tossed blond hair, relaxed poses on a rawhide couch, or peppering her vocabulary with southern expressions could totally mask her steel core.

"You know, if you get this job, you and I will spend most of our time together," Gail purred, flipping a lock of hair over her jean-jacketed shoulder. "You will be half of my brain," she leaned in. "This position is *hhuge-ly* important to me." I nodded and scrawled hasty notes. "*Millions* of details go into making a movie, and each choice — like the exact shade of blood on a wall, or the shadow under Kate Hudson's nose — each tiny detail has to be *right* and has to be *tracked,*" Gail continued as I scribbled.

She looked up at a stuffed deer head on the wall, then back at me. "You'll be responsible for *continuity* — do you know what that means?" Gail didn't wait for a response. "*Seemingly,* seemingly insignificant details have to be perfect — and consistent! — over the course of *months* of production. Sometimes two years!"

My ball-point pen flew across the page, leaving a stream of partial words — Gail's words. "And then there's editing. EDITING!" Gail's boot heels landed on the floor with a thud. "That's where things can *really* get fucked. But you'll handle it." The air conditioner hummed in the background. I noticed my fingers were cold and squeezed my bare legs together. "What I'm saying is, there's *no* room for error. The stakes are *way* too high." Gail leaned toward me and raised her eyebrows as if to say, *"You got it?"*

Before this second interview, the legendary producer had arranged for me to meet one of her assistants. The casually dressed, slightly overweight young woman had said matter-of- factly that Gail was a perfectionist who sometimes got angry. "But if you take it home with you, that's *your* problem," she said, spinning around slowly in her office chair. "Screamers" were ubiquitous in Hollywood — part of the culture — but there were degrees ranging from mild, to survivable, to toxic, to outright abusive. As the hiring process seemed to be moving quickly, I felt like I needed to bring up a real issue. "Gail," I said, "I'm truly excited to be considered for this role. I think I should tell you, though, I've never done a job exactly like this before."

Gail froze. The room went silent. It felt like time had stopped. The antique grandfather clock counted seconds in the corner. *Tick. Tock. Tick...*

Then, anger exploded across Gail's face. Her skin turned crimson. Throwing up her hands, she said, "Well, if you're not confident in yourself, there's nothing I can do about it!" Gail smacked her hands on her thighs in exasperation. She stood up, turned on her boot heels, and stomped loudly away from me.

"But, Gail..." I stammered, "I *am* confident...! I just want to be totally honest!" I pleaded, watching the back of her tiny figure recede in the distance. Gail slammed an antique Texas door behind her before I could finish my thought. In expressing the truth about my lack of experience to ensure that Gail understood a risk of hiring me, I had stepped on a landmine. Bang! I was history. On my way out, I looked at the administrative assistant I had met as if to say, "What just happened?" She shrugged and took a bite of her candy bar as if to say, "Welcome to our world." I never heard from Gail again.

You could call this "blowing the interview." I had been on a path to landing a job offer until I made a statement that the employer didn't like. Did I sabotage myself?

In my view, I saved myself. I saw a level of anger that I would never want to experience in the workplace — or anywhere. If this Hollywood icon could get so upset about my making an honest statement of concern during our interview — the "seduction" phase when everyone is putting their best foot forward — I could only imagine how blistering her personality might be when I made a mistake on the job, which I knew would be inevitable, given the "*millions* of details" and "high stakes" involved.

The comment from the assistant, that Gail was known to get angry, "but if you take it home with you, that's your problem," echoed in my head. In the coming days, while I still wanted OUT of my grueling job at the agency as soon as humanly possible, I felt that I had dodged a bullet.

More often, warning signs pop up during the hiring process that you can only see clearly in hindsight. In one such process at a large company, I got the feeling that the CEO of the organization wanted his vice president to bring me onto the team. How did I know? During my interview with him while meeting other executives, he said with a slight wink, "We're going to work this out. You'll be terrific here."

During the negotiation of the details of the job offer, I realized that the vice president had to get approval from the CEO on every detail we discussed — compensation, benefits, my title, etc. The CEO was directing the hiring process, but was out of the picture once I was hired. Then, the vice president seemed displeased with everything I did. I couldn't master technical processes like she did with professorial zeal. Like her boss the CEO, I was a strategic people person, not a technical expert like the VP. Almost from the first day, "Shirin" was unhappy with me. For two years, she tried, and finally succeeded, in firing me. I might have avoided those nightmarish 25 months had I been looking harder for warning signs in the interview process.

The goal of an interview is to advance to the next stage — another interview, a job offer, etc. While you may be observing pluses and minuses of the opportunity during the interview process, the goal is usually to get a job offer. Once you have a job offer, you can decide whether to negotiate aspects like compensation, location, and benefits, and ultimately whether or not to accept the offer.

How to Prepare for a Job Interview

- Research the people you will be meeting and any recent news about or press releases the organization has posted.
- Scope out the location in advance — parking, the entrance, etc.
- Practice, practice, practice answering expected interview questions — especially the hard ones like "What are your weaknesses?" Ask a friend to drill with you.
- Dress appropriately.
- Arrive 10-15 minutes early.
- Go to the restroom, look in the mirror. Straighten your hair and clothes. Avoid heavy perfume and after-shave.
- If you are waiting in the reception area and expecting the hiring manager to emerge, arrange your belongings so you can easily stand up and greet the hiring manager when he or she approaches, rather than having to juggle your coat, bag, briefcase, etc.
- Bring several hard copies of your resume.
- Bring your business cards.

The Personal Touch

Since the interview is largely about personality "fit," part of your preparation should be to research the people you will be meeting in the interview. Ask whomever is scheduling your meetings for all their names and look them up on the internet. You might find that someone attended a school you went to. Or that one of the executives is involved in a charitable organization, for instance. People love to be recognized and complimented, so it's good to use the opportunity in an interview to compliment or recognize something in the background of your interviewers. For example, "I saw that you graduated with honors from William & Mary. That's really impressive." Or, "I noticed that you served on the board of So Others Might Eat. What a great organization." Then, let them talk. Recognizing someone for an accomplishment tends to be a good conversation starter, and shows you have done your homework — another desirable quality to demonstrate.

Whenever you are communicating with potential employers — including on your resume, in a cover letter, or in an interview — one of the best strategies I know is to describe your abilities and interests in ways that put the employer's interests first. In other words, rather than, "I want to develop my international marketing skills," frame the sentence this way: "My Spanish language and marketing experience will enable me to hit the ground running to expand global sales."

In the way you communicate, show that you understand the organization's priorities and success are paramount. Doing so, you convey to the hiring manager that you understand that your role is to advance the organization, not just build your career.

For example:

Before: "I am a product manager with eight years of experience in large banks managing multiple product development teams. In addition, I have an MBA with a focus on strategy, and speak fluent French and Spanish. I would like to develop my international product development skills and finance skills."

After: "My product management experience will be useful in mobilizing the teams here to solve problems and innovate solutions. My fluency in both Spanish and French would be helpful in communicating with the team. The company is well positioned to take growth to a new level, and I am eager to lead that effort."

The "Before" example is a list of skills, degrees, and experiences. The "After" example shows how those assets would be useful to the organization, and that you, the candidate, understand that the employer's goals are what count.

Answering the hardest questions

You can anticipate some of the questions that will emerge during a job interview, and should prepare for them. One deceptively simple and predictable question that you should prepare for is, "Tell me about yourself."

"You said to start my presentation with a joke, so I showed them my paycheck."

Glasbergen

The challenge in answering this question effectively is to determine how much you should say, and what should you emphasize. Your answer shouldn't be too long, but this is a moment to talk a bit about your background and who you are, as well as advancing the concept that you are a good candidate for the job. When answering this question, you want to start to lay out the narrative of your candidacy — why you are a good candidate for the position.

I typically start with where I grew up and how some of my interests started to develop as a young person. I briefly summarize sections of my work history to spend more time on the most relevant portions of my career for the job I'm seeking, and try to blend actual titles and specific jobs with overall themes. I don't want to talk for too long in response to any given question, so it's important to highlight relevant facts while getting through your personal timeline in a brief way. *Rehearse a two-minute answer to this question.* The story may be a little different for different jobs. Also, as you are answering, reference relevant points you found in your research of the interviewers. For instance, "I joined the Girl Scouts in second grade and became very active. I noticed you serve on the board of the Charlotte chapter..."

How to answer "What are your weaknesses?"

"How would you describe your weaknesses?" is a standard interview question. "How would you describe your areas for growth?" is the same question using more nuanced language. Prepare for this question. Your biggest weakness may be your lack of confidence, or narcissistic tendencies, or lack of trust in others, but it's dangerous to be completely honest about our deepest flaws in a job interview. In truth, this question is asked in order to determine whether a candidate demonstrates some degree of self-awareness and whether he or she can communicate succinctly about areas for development. Keeping in mind, of course, that a prospective employer may already have an opinion as to what your weaknesses (on paper) are relative to the perceived "ideal" candidate. Because of the nature of the hiring process, the employer's perception of your "weaknesses" may not ever be stated.

Generally candidates point to an "acceptable" flaw like "I'm a perfectionist" or "I care too much" or "I have very high expectations." One approach is to be candid about an area in which you would like to improve. Another strategy is to identify experience gaps relevant to the role being discussed. For instance, "I've never worked in the international nonprofit sector before." Or, "I don't have a finance background, but I love steep learning curves."

The main objective is to share something that is true without disqualifying yourself. The best answer is credible, brief, and indicates that you are interested in improving and growing.

Here are Indeed.com's Top Ten best answers to "What is your biggest weakness?"[20]

1. I focus too much on the details.
2. I have a hard time letting go of a project.
3. I have trouble saying "no."
4. I get impatient when projects run beyond the deadline.
5. I could use more experience in...
6. I sometimes lack confidence.
7. I can have trouble asking for help.
8. It has been difficult for me to work with certain personalities.

9. It can be difficult for me to maintain a healthy work/life balance.

10. In the past I have been uncomfortable with ambiguity.

Practice your answers to challenging interview questions with friends or colleagues.

Because most of us don't interview every month or every year, practice when you're starting a job search. Do mock interviews with friends. Rehearse answering the tough questions several times in the mirror. Ask for advice. By the time you get to the interview, you will be more confident, relaxed, and able to let your personality and talents shine.

What to wear to an interview

Changing norms in dress codes have thrown a monkey wrench into choosing clothes for job interviews. "I sent a candidate into a major food manufacturer for a maintenance manager position," recruiter Al Molson of The Colonial Group told *The Wall Street Journal.*[21] The candidate showed up "wearing a Nascar racing jacket with the name of the sponsor — Viagra — in big letters. I was dumfounded. I had spent 30 minutes telling this guy what to wear. He said he didn't have a suit. I told him to get one." The candidate didn't land the job.

The bottom line is, you want to feel confident and look professional when you interview. Make sure your hair is clean, not in need of a haircut, and styled in a way you like. For most office jobs, you should look business-like and dressed like the others. A job interview is not the time to show your wild side. Avoid heavy cologne or perfume! You don't want to be exed-out because your wardrobe choices stood out in a way that said, "I'm not a fit for this environment."

For women, to state the obvious, don't show cleavage. While too much body and tattoo exposure are normal in casual dress, they are not appropriate in job interviews. Similarly, in shoe choice, err on the side of dressy (but not nightclubby or sexy) as opposed to casual. While you want to look sharp and professional, you don't want your five-inch heels, your tats, your manicure, or your breasts to draw attention.

"Years ago, I worked as a consultant for professional membership organization in New Jersey, and I was screening job candidates for an executive administrative-assistant position," another recruiter, Jonathan Schiff of Fairleigh Dickinson University, told the *Journal*.[22] "One of the candidates was a fairly recent Harvard grad with a terrific resume. The day of her interview she showed up wearing a full Elizabethan theatrical outfit, including makeup. She was very interested in the job, and she mentioned that the reason why she came in like this is she wanted anyone who hired her to know that her first love is really for the theater. I did not recommend her for the job."

"You're kidding. I thought it was Friday."

cartoonstock.com

For men, wearing a tie shows respect, even if workplace dress codes don't demand one for most occasions. In general, err on the side of professional, rather than casual, for the interview wardrobe. Your clothing should convey that you can be part of a team and that *you want to be hired.*

Beverages and snacks

A typical start to the interview is to be asked whether you would like coffee or water. Even if you're not thirsty, say yes to water or something simple. If your host says, "We have a great coffee machine and lots of choices," go ahead and accept even if you're unsure. Think of being a guest in someone's house: when hospitality is offered, it's a nice gesture to accept. And doing so right away creates a joint activity that makes everyone feel less like strangers. The result can be conversation that helps everyone get to know each other in an innocuous way.

Power move: After the interview, pick up your water bottle, cup, etc. and dispose of it. Cleaning up after yourself is a subtle way to show that you know good manners and are part of the team, rather than leaving it to others to pick up after you.

Thank you notes

After the interview, whether you want the job or not, a thank-you email within 24 hours is standard. Keep it short, warm, and factual, not a catalogue of your qualifications. And send it fast — later in the day or the very next morning! Signal your enthusiasm. Really wanting the job (in a positive, not desperate way) counts...

Examples from TheMuse.com, a job and career site:

Sample #1

Dear Javier,

Thank you so much for chatting with me today. It was such a pleasure to learn more about the marketing manager role, and I'm very excited about the opportunity to join News Crew and help your team bring a new readership to your amazing content.

I look forward to hearing from you about next steps, but please don't hesitate to contact me if I can provide any additional information.

All the best,
Liz

Liz Sample
Address
Email
Phone

Sample #2

This example is more personal and detailed, and reminds the hiring manager of your skills and enthusiasm:

Hi Ms. Bernard,

I just wanted to thank you for inviting me to your office today. It was great to hear about 4Apps' goals for streamlining your software and placing an emphasis on quality UX design, and how you see the engineering department playing a role in these initiatives. 4Apps seems like a wonderful place to work—and not just because you mentioned some great summer outings! I really admire the mission that drives your business, and look forward to the opportunity to work with your team to implement some of the ideas I mentioned around redesigning the homepage.

Please let me know if there is anything else you need from me to move the process forward.

Have a great rest of your week,
Koo Vinson

Another way to demonstrate your interest and skills is to include a few ideas to follow up on topics discussed during the interview. The risk is that your ideas will show the interviewer that your skills don't match up with the job opening. On the other hand, showing the initiative of generating follow-up ideas — emphasizing that they are ideas for discussion — demonstrates enthusiasm, initiative, and follow-through — key attributes for which all employers yearn:

Sample #3

Dear Namdi,

Thank you so much for meeting with me today. I really enjoyed learning more about your career trajectory at CarRuns (and hearing what it was like to join as the fifth employee—so impressive!) and where you see the company going in the next few years.

To follow up on our conversation about client retention, I've attached a short deck I mocked up with my initial ideas for increasing renewals. Happy to discuss further if you think useful.

I can tell CarRuns is a special place to work and would be thrilled to join such an innovative, hardworking, and passionate team of individuals. Please let me know if there is anything else I can provide to make your hiring decision easier.

Best regards,
Anika Johnson

Another way to make an impression is to drop a second, handwritten note in the mail — snail mail. Obviously, choose different words than you used in your email. Use nice-quality stationary, like Crane's, which you can find in a card shop or office supply store. When it comes to thank-you notes, whether you go simple, more elaborate, or the extra mile with a handwritten note, the main thing is, don't skip the thank-you note! It's an essential demonstration of your professionalism, workplace readiness, and manners. You never know what small difference is going to score you the offer ahead of all the other qualified candidates.

Bottom line, landing a job interview is a great success. Congratulations! Now you have a chance to check out a new organization, meet new people, and shine. Most of all, demonstrate that you want to be hired! You can always reject a job offer after receiving one. Enthusiasm during the entire process is critical. Prepare, prepare, prepare so you can be relaxed and enjoy the experience.

Generations at Work

I rarely do interviews with entry-level candidates since our company now has more than 500 people. But a friend asked me if I would interview his sister's son as a courtesy, so I said yes. He had a degree from a decent college and did a good job in the interview. At the end, after about a half hour, I said, "So what do you think?" He said, "Working here would be good — as a first step in my career." We didn't hire him.

VIMAL, ASSET MANAGEMENT COMPANY CO-FOUNDER

Millennials have long been the butt of jokes told by their predecessors in the workplace. They have been lampooned for acting entitled, lazy, naïve — a generation attached at the hip to their parents, the Baby Boomers. But now, Millennials — that massive wave of 75 million Americans born between 1981 and 1996 (there are 2 billion Millennials worldwide) — are becoming more and more dominant as they rise up the workplace ladder. Today, as Millennials move into management positions (the oldest Millennials turned 43 in 2024), they are instituting an array of employment and hiring policies "that would have been unheard of at a workplace run by earlier generations," according to MuchSkills, a management consulting firm.[23] What's in, according to the consultants:

- remote work
- learning at work
- reskilling opportunities
- skilled freelancers filling skill gaps
- flexible teams
- continuous feedback
- transparency and collaboration

What's out:

- the traditional 9-5 office routine
- performance reviews
- the Monday-Friday in-person workweek

Also, Millennials and Gen Zers — the generation following Millennials — change jobs a lot. Gen Z joined the workforce just as the pandemic upended all the standard operating procedures. Not surprisingly, that's changed the way this young cohort views work, with Gen Z showing a greater willingness to job hop than older generations. Members of Gen Z switch jobs at a rate 134 percent higher than in 2019, according to LinkedIn. That compares to 24 percent of Millennials who switched jobs more than in 2019, and 4 percent less for Boomers. Gen Zers plan to keep moving: 25 percent told LinkedIn said they hope or plan to leave their employers in the first six months of 2023, compared with 23 percent of Millennials.[24]

In short, the incoming and increasingly dominant generations in the workplace change jobs more often, making the workplace more transitory for everyone. Why? Because organizations, more and more reliant on technology, have adapted by making onboarding (and termination) systematic and fast. The more prepared companies are for rapid turnover, the more it happens. Technology enables and encourages churn.

> *McDonald's told corporate employees to stay home for three days in early 2023 so the company could avoid in-person terminations of hundreds of workers. "The Chicago-based fast-food chain said in an internal email last week to U.S. employees and some international staff that they should work from home from Monday through Wednesday so it can deliver staffing decisions virtually. The company, in the message, asked employees to cancel all in-person meetings with vendors and other outside parties at its headquarters." The company said, "During the week of April 3, we will communicate key decisions related to roles and staffing levels across the organization."*
>
> ***The Wall Street Journal*, April 2023**

Large amounts of remote work often fuel isolation and burnout, reducing satisfaction and fulfillment at work that may spur the desire to switch. Yet, Millennials and Gen Zers — post-pandemic — adapted to remote work and now want the option to open their laptops wherever they are. "We can't get our teams to come back to the office," said one HR manager of a tech company in 2023. "Those who live locally point to their colleagues in other countries, working remotely, and say, 'If they can work from home, why can't I?'" Another HR chief at a global financial software company warned her bosses in Zurich that if they mandated a three-days-in-the-office policy, "more than 25 percent of our staff would walk out the door." As discussed earlier, job changes often involve a salary increase, whereas staying put in many organizations means wage stagnation. Seen in this way, Millennials' and Gen Zers' serial job-hopping is both rational, and significant.

Boomers to Gen Z

At the other end of the workforce age range, Baby Boomers (born 1946 to 1964) and Gen Xers (born 1965 to 1980) are staying in the workforce longer and creating a dynamic of their own. The last two U.S. presidents started office in their late 70s. U.S. Secretary of the Treasury Janet Yellen was recruited to the job at the age of 74. The inimitable Henry Kissinger was still in the game after his 100th birthday.

Whereas, at one time, women hit their peak working years before age 50 and men by 60, these days, working into one's 60s or 70s is becoming more and more common. Millennials and Gen Zers' embrace — and the pandemic's expansion of remote work — accelerated the trend. A 2020 survey by Voya Financial found that 59 percent of employed Baby Boomers plan to work during retirement, as well as 60 percent of Generation X and nearly half (49 percent) of Millennials. [25]

According to a study by global consulting firm Bain & Company, older experienced workers will make up more than a quarter of the workforce by 2031. "That's a massive shift," Andrew Schwedel, partner at Bain & Company, told CNBC's *Squawk Box*.[26] According to data in the survey "a long-term trend toward *earlier retirement* is slowly going into reverse." The spike in retirements during the early months of the pandemic now looks more like "a Great Sabbatical," Bain said.

The U.S. Bureau of Labor Statistics predicts the shift to happen even sooner, estimating that by the year 2028, 25 percent of the workforce will be workers over the age of 55. [27] People are living and working longer. Bain said retirees are rejoining the labor force, driven by a hot job market, inflation, and reduced Covid-related health risks. Also, the lack of pensions, retirement savings, and later eligibility for government retirement benefits play a role. One can start receiving Social Security as early as age 62, but collecting at that age means a lower monthly payment for life. Full benefits come at what Social Security calls your "full retirement age" — 67. If you delay taking your benefits until reaching age 70, benefits increase.[28] In 2021, 39 percent of people over 55 were employed or looking for work.

Where do they fit in? Corporations want employees who are reliable, perform well, adapt, and communicate skillfully. The pandemic may have increased opportunities for older workers who don't necessarily need on-the-job basic training and have a level of maturity and broad range of skills younger workers usually lack. Older workers need to be comfortable with technology and social media, and prepare to learn new workplace practices. The upside is that while COVID was toughest on the oldest among us, the changes that the pandemic brought to the work place may actually help older workers for a long time to come.

So, while the rise of Millennial and Gen Z bosses will likely mean increased turnover and less stability in the workplace, the dominance of these younger generations may open expanded opportunities for older workers.

Some employers are already shifting recruiting efforts to find older workers. "The main problem we face is that younger people who want to work here, the first question they ask is, 'What's the work-life balance?'" laments Ivo, CEO of a technology firm outside Duesseldorf, Germany. The company goes to great lengths to recruit and retain technology workers, including offering a standard hiring bonus of a *new car* for all employees! But those and other perks haven't solved a problem most employers report: younger workers who focus excessively on protecting time off.

Over all, nearly three-quarters (74 percent) of 1,000 managers and business leaders surveyed by website Resume Builder said they find Gen Z (workers under 25) to be more difficult than other generations to work with, with nearly half (49 percent) saying they find it difficult to work with Gen Z employees all or most of the time. [29]

Solana, a national political organizer, faced similar issues when recruiting for full-time environmental campaigner roles that paid $90,000 per year. "What do you mean by full-time?" numerous candidates asked Solana. "Will I be expected to work more than 40 hours a week?" Needless to say, those candidates didn't make the cut. Some who did washed out during their first year. Many Gen Z candidates "first want to know what our 'Friday policy' is," one technology executive laughs. "Is it a full day? Is it a remote day? Is it a fun day?" As a result, the executive says, his company is hiring more software engineers in their 50s.

Joe, who owns a popular bicycle shop in Maine, pays high school freshmen a starting salary of $18 per hour to work in his busy store. The shop's expansive sales floor features hundreds of bikes of all kinds. Joe said:

> *We have all the business in the world but there just isn't enough affordable housing here, so it is hard to find employees. We are building housing for our team members but we can't build it fast enough. One kid who worked for us from the beginning of high school through college, part-time — we gave him a brand new two-bedroom apartment with oak floors for $300/ month. He was making $25/hour and $50-60 a day in tips. On*

July 2, he said, "I'm leaving in three days to go to Europe with my girlfriend for two weeks." There was no negotiation. That's the busiest time of the year in our store. When he came back, I said, "I'm sorry, but we don't need you here anymore." It's sad — the lack of work ethic in young people here. The first thing they ask is, "How much are you going to pay me?"

"Next year," Joe said, "I'm going to hire retirees. See that guy over there? He's in his 50s. He shows up before the rest of us in the morning and he leaves after everyone else. He loves working and he is great with customers, getting things done. We gave him a subsidized apartment. He makes $25/hour. He is so happy to be here. He is a rockstar. I'm looking for people like that."

"I tell these kids, we really have an opportunity to make a difference in someone's day," Joe, the bicycle store owner, continued. Our customers show up here with bikes they haven't used in five years. They may be frustrated. We can turn that situation around. We can really save a vacation. I say, 'Just give them a rental bike and see if we can fix the problem by the time they get back from a day on the trails.' It's an amazing opportunity. Customers come back and they're so grateful. We don't advertise because our clients keep coming back. We have way more business than we need." With strong work ethic and maturity, could older employees hold the winning cards in the workplace of the future? At the end of the day, people who work hard will succeed.

What about ageism?

"In an interview I had, the hiring manager said, 'I think you'd be a great addition to our team, because there are three women, and you could mentor them,'" reports Sandra, who found herself back in the job market at 60 after tech layoffs, where she was a sales executive. "I'm confronting ageism, yes," Sandra continued. "One job board I subscribe to had a webinar on how to make yourself look younger on your resume. Part of that was language. Not using certain language in your cover letter, etc. Also, removing the year you graduated. The presenter said, 'Don't show more than 10 years of experience on your resume.' I don't like it but I understanding why they're saying it."

"You were right, Mom. Having you there made it a much nicer annual review."

cartoonstock.com

Sandra is pragmatic — her LinkedIn profile now includes only the last ten years of her multi-decade work history. She includes her full set of experiences on her (offline) resume, which she uses in interviews — after she has passed through algorithmic filters and is in discussions with real humans. Recruiters say they like to see job seekers' abbreviated *and* full profiles. Both are useful — like a two-minute overview video vs. a full-length documentary. Be practical — prepare both.

The truth is, no matter what employers say about desiring workers of all ages, ageism exists. Until this discrimination is eradicated, older job seekers should be savvy. Being active on social media and developing strong technology and communications skills are vital. As Estée Lauder's CEO, Fabrizio Freda, told the *Harvard Business Review*, the company "had come to a place where the future could not be informed by the past" and therefore decided to implement a reverse mentoring program in which older and younger workers are paired and counsel each other on workplace challenges. The trend is gaining popularity not just because it helps older executives, but also because "reverse-mentoring programs provide Millennials with the transparency and recognition that they're seeking from management," according to *HBR*. [30]

If you are confronting ageism in the job market, consider asking for help from a Millennial or Gen Zer. Young people feel elevated and empowered when they help older adults. Listening to their counsel you help yourself — and them.

Quiz: What is the one thing workers of every age need to better navigate this choppy new landscape? Financial security. All of us need to start building it now.

The Frugal Fabulous: Long-term Strategies for Financial Security and Freedom

In the moments after you have lost your job, you feel bruised, battered and beaten up. You probably feel scared. Where is the money going to come from? What about the mortgage, the bills? Most organizations offer some kind of severance package — a sum of money and possibly benefits — in exchange for your signing a non-disclosure agreement (NDA) when you lose your job.

As challenging as this situation is, you need to steel yourself and argue as effectively as you can for as much severance pay as possible. "If you are dismissed, take notes during the termination meeting [if you are given one] and don't feel pressured to sign the severance agreement immediately. Stall for time to review the document and think it through. Typically, you will have 21 days to accept the agreement, and once it's signed, you have seven days to change your mind," according to Investopedia, the financial information website. [31]

After an initial review of the severance agreement, you may decide to hire an employment law attorney especially if you have evidence of discrimination, if the language in the package is too complicated or broad, or if the agreement is multiple pages long, says Investopedia. "Ask the lawyer which state laws govern severance agreements and if specific stipulations exist regarding timing and payment amounts," Investopedia advises. If you are a senior executive, or are in a "protected class," the help of an attorney may be well worth the cost. What is a "protected class?" Under federal law, "applicants, employees, and former employees are protected from employment discrimination based on race, color, religion, sex (including pregnancy, sexual orientation, or gender identity), national origin, age (40 or older), disability and genetic information (including family medical history), states the Equal Employment Opportunity Commission. [32] If you can't hire an attorney, you must represent yourself as powerfully as possible, bringing forth arguments based on reason *and* emotion. An appeal for more severance pay should be grounded in such facts as:

- Precedent at the organization — has the organization offered severance packages before? You can argue for more money based on relevant precedents. Some organizations have a policy of offering one month's severance for every year employed.
- Market conditions — how is the job market, how long will you need to secure a new position with similar compensation? Ask a recruiter or placement agency.
- Your record of service — a severance request should underscore your service and commitment to the organization, *appealing to your employer's emotions and sense of fairness.* In this challenging time, a personal email to the CEO or the most

senior person in the organization can make a difference.

"The salary is excellent and the benefits are outstanding.
So... which would you prefer?"

cartoonstock.com

When one senior position I held for a year was suddenly "eliminated," a personal email to the CEO who originally hired me resulted in a four-month consulting contract that did tide me over for weeks while I was unemployed and even continued after my next new job landed. The consulting assignment didn't involve much work. Instead, I believe the contract was offered so the CEO could justify a larger payout to me, because she knew the organization bore responsibility for the chaos that had resulted in my being jobless.

In addition to severance pay, do your utmost to secure health insurance coverage for a few months. Smaller employers can be more flexible on these points; larger employers usually have set internal procedures and policies. Those policies can be adjusted if someone senior enough in the organization demands it. Send your appeals to the top.

This sample letter to the CEO of a small organization from the administrative assistant she terminated combines well-written facts with an emotional appeal:

Dear Kayla,

I am writing you personally to ask for your consideration regarding a separation agreement following my unexpected termination last week.

After 15 months of 24/7 attention to my job, many lost hours of sleep when I was on the phone late at night or before dawn making sure you got where you needed to go and had everything you needed, it was gut wrenching and totally traumatizing to be told I was fired and then — without any contact with you — led, like a criminal, to the exit.

This is the worst professional experience of my life. From the day I started at Firm X, I jumped on every assignment you gave me. I took a proactive approach to the job — always looking for ways to make your life easier and your working time as effective as possible. I cleaned your desk, Kayla, and did my best every day to support you in any way I could. I worked on weekends, and as you know volunteered to help LaTonya's team at recent board meetings. I slept very little or not at all during those events. To me this approach to the job was due to my loyalty and commitment to you — I gave you my very best performance to the best of my ability every single day.

It was baffling, hurtful and heart-stopping to be told last week, without warning, that I "didn't take ownership" of my role. Thinking about the last 15 months, I honestly can't imagine how I could have taken any more ownership. This cloaked language leaves me feeling even more demoralized. How can I do better the next time in my next job without real facts and honest communication? The treatment i received is shameful. I am shocked that you would countenance this behavior by your staff.

Based on my dedication to you and Firm X, and the clear precedent of offering 4-6 months of severance support to those caught in turnover-producing personnel decisions (Carlos Diaz, Betsy Dyer, and Sangeeta Patel, to name a few), I would respectfully ask that Firm X offer me at least a three-month severance to help mitigate the devastation of this situation, both financially and professionally. It will be all I can do to explain these circumstances to a prospective employer — your firing of me without even a week's notice will have a severe effect on my ability to get another job.

I ask you to act with humanity in a terrible situation.

Tipli Barnes

After a negotiation with Human Resources, Tipli secured eight weeks of severance pay and three months of health insurance coverage — not bad for a 15-month run at Firm X. Organizations offer severance packages to enhance their reputations and reduce negative fallout from terminations and layoffs. Individuals who carry out terminations are humans who, like most of us, don't like causing harm to others and the associated feelings of guilt. Take advantage of those factors.

Key takeaways on negotiating severance when terminated:

- Most employers offer a severance agreement that defines the financial terms upon which an employee will leave a company when their employment is terminated.

- Severance agreements are not required by law, but employers tend to offer them as gestures of goodwill or to be competitive in their industries.
- Continuation of insurance benefits, assistance finding another job, and other perks can also be negotiated as a severance agreement.
- Typical severance packages offer one to two weeks of paid salary for every year worked.
- You usually have 21 days to accept a severance agreement, and once it's signed, you have seven days to change your mind.[33]

Dear Kayla,

I am writing you personally to ask for your consideration regarding a separation agreement following my unexpected termination last week.

After 15 months of 24/7 attention to my job, many lost hours of sleep when I was on the phone late at night or before dawn making sure you got where you needed to go and had everything you needed, it was gut wrenching and totally traumatizing to be told I was fired and then — without any contact with you — led, like a criminal, to the exit.

This is the worst professional experience of my life. From the day I started, I jumped on every assignment you gave me. I took a proactive approach to the job — always looking for ways to make your life easier and your working time as effective as possible. I cleaned your desk, Kayla, and did my best every day to support you in any way I could. I worked on weekends, and as you know volunteered to help LaTonya's team at recent board meetings. I slept very little or not at all during those events. To me this approach to the job was due to my loyalty and commitment to you — I gave you my very best performance to the best of my ability every single day.

It was baffling, hurtful and heart-stopping to be told last week, without warning, that I "didn't take ownership" of my role. Thinking about the last 15 months, I honestly can't imagine how I could have taken any more ownership. This cloaked language leaves me feeling even more demoralized. How can I do better the next time in my next job without real facts and honest communication? The treatment I received is shameful. I am shocked that you would countenance this behavior by your staff.

Based on my dedication to you and our team, and the clear precedent of offering 4-6 months of severance support to those caught in turnover-producing personnel decisions (Carlos Diaz, Betsy Dyer, and Sangeeta Patel, to name a few), I would respectfully ask that you offer me at least a three-month severance to help mitigate the devastation of this situation, both financially and professionally. It will be all I can do to explain these circumstances to a prospective employer — your firing of me without even a week's notice will have a severe effect on my ability to get another job.

I ask you to act with humanity in a terrible situation.

Tipli Barnes

make it personal

clear topic sentence

specific

long hours!

emotional effect

visual

desired workplace qualities

desire to improve

point to precedent

reference as many others as possible

specific request

emphasize harshness

point to a better approach

Benefits Packages

Some employers include severance guidelines in the benefits package included in the employment offer. Before you accept a position, make sure to ask for a detailed review of benefits. A basic benefits package should include:

- Health benefits
- Retirement benefits
- Paid time off
- As Millennials take over management roles, flexible schedules and the ability to work remotely may become more common elements of benefits packages.

After you receive a job offer, there may be room to negotiate to increase your compensation and/or improve benefits. Negotiating during the "offer stage" of the hiring process has become more common, almost expected. If you negotiate, be humble and marshal facts. Why? The risk is that you can turn off an employer by seeming to overestimate your value. If you appeal for more money, keep the request modest — usually not more than five to 10 percent of the offered compensation. If your request is refused, be magnanimous and ask for a salary review in six months. Think of what you can request that won't cost the employer money. Title enhancements and flexible scheduling are good examples. But the bottom line is, if you want the role you have been offered, you should maintain the positive and collaborative tone you want to continue when you're on board. In the long term, a reputation for hard work, loyalty, and collegiality (including putting the interests of team, not yourself, first) will result in higher compensation, better benefits and greater opportunities than the small enhancements you can negotiate in a job offer.

HR Professional Padmakar Gunjal offers these key tips for negotiating benefits on LinkedIn:

- Be flexible; don't get hung up on trivial issues, and always seek compromise when possible. Anticipate objections and prepare effective answers to these objections.
- Remain enthusiastic and upbeat even if the negotiations get a little hot. This might be your first test under fire. Play hardball only if you're willing to walk away from, or lose, the deal.
- Be sure to get the offer and final agreement in writing. You should feel comfortable asking the employer for 24 to 48 hours to think about the deal if you need time to think it over.
- Never link salary to personal needs or problems. Compensation should always be linked to your value.[34]

Building Financial Security

Now that you know how to handle negotiations at the beginning and end of an assignment, how do you build financial security in the long term?

Marie was a newly-minted MBA working in her first job at a large regional bank in Charlotte, North Carolina. Marie liked to look good at work — not to be flashy but to appear stylish and professional. Spending money on good clothes was worthwhile, she told herself. She was investing in her professional success, supporting her climb up the ladder. "How much of your salary are you saving?" I asked her one day as she swiveled her chair behind a modern desk, sitting in front of a floor-to-ceiling window in the bank's skyscraper offices. "I don't save anything," she admitted sheepishly. "I spend all my extra money on bags and shoes." Marie's spending habits, while extreme, are not altogether unusual. Over the long term, however, they are financially disastrous.

First of all, everyone needs a six-month rainy day fund to cover costs in the event of job loss. But that's just the beginning. Sometimes, we need to be reminded many times before putting sound financial habits into practice. In my late thirties, as I slaved away in a Hollywood talent agency at a glamorous sounding job that paid minimum wage, my dear mother bugged me about my finances. Finally she said, "You need a pension, Beth." She repeated this declaration, which was really a plea, on our frequent coast-to-coast calls. "A *pension?*" I laughed. "No one has a pension anymore, Mom." I rolled my eyes. Only a few government workers and ancient corporate executives had pensions, I told her. The era of pensions was over — didn't she know? But dear Mom kept after me. "You need to *save* for when you *can't work* anymore. You need money for *later in life*," she begged sweetly.

She wasn't saying, "You need a husband" as some parents pressured their daughters (Thank God!). In fact, the last thing she wanted was for me to feel forced to marry to establish financial security. "Don't compromise," she said instead. "Value your independence." But she was insistent that I start building my own financial foundation for the long term.

Mom's words had gone in one ear and out the other many times before, but one Sunday as I was wandering through an expensive Beverly Hills department store, admiring a beautiful designer sandal costing three-figures, it suddenly dawned on me that slapping down my credit card for these chic concoctions would be like lighting a match under a pile of greenbacks, burning the money in my bank account. Suddenly, the fun went out of "retail therapy" faster than a Lamborghini speeding down Sunset Boulevard.

What happened? Something clicked. Mom had always said that a dollar saved was worth *more* than a dollar earned. Suddenly I viewed my unnecessary spending like pulling the rug out from under a solid financial future — not to mention financial *security!*

Let me explain Mom's theory that "a dollar saved is worth more than a dollar earned." When you earn a dollar at work, the government slices off its share for federal taxes, state taxes, Medicare, Social Security, etc. etc. For most people, take home pay only amounts to 72 percent of their gross income — not including expenses like health insurance.

On the other hand, a dollar saved, left alone, gains worth. These days, dollars saved in bank earn decent interest. During periods of low interest rates, if you start to invest in stocks and mutual funds, your money grows on average at about eight percent per year. Sometimes, more. Depending on interest rates, Certificates of Deposit (CDs) at banks and government offerings like Treasury notes and bonds can be solid, lucrative savings vehicles. Developing a habit of paying off debts and investing your money — building *financial discipline* — is literally the ticket to freedom and being able to make the choices you want throughout your life.

That day I placed an expensive sandal back on its acrylic pedestal, doing so didn't exactly feel like saving much money, but it was the start of a new habit: trimming my expenses. I stopped dropping big bucks on clothes and accessories I didn't need. Sometimes, I used a trick. If I really liked something that seemed less than necessary, I would tell myself I could come back for it the next day if I really wanted it. How many times did I actually do that? Zero. For me, delaying the gratification of the spending impulse made it go away.

What will work for you? In a word, you have to spend less and save more. Every so-called "strategy" boils down to this simple truth.

In *Badass Habits, New York Times* bestselling author and life coach Jen Sincero writes:

> *Let's say you've tried over and over to break your habit of spending more than you make. You've got a well-paying job and you put part of each paycheck toward your credit card bill and a little into your savings account and you carefully map out your budget each month. Then, in spite of your careful planning, you find yourself going on trips and forensically investigating furniture sales and jovially shouting, "Drinks are on me!" and before you know it, your savings account is a ghost town and you're pleading on the phone with Pat at the collection agency again. Chances are excellent that deep down you're scared to stop overspending because you're trying to fill an emotional hole with stuff and experiences.*[35]

Breaking bad habits and forming good practices is easier if you realize why the old habits formed in the first place. The key is not to judge your coping mechanisms, but to see them, to observe, not to beat up on yourself, but to realize you want a more solid financial foundation to stand on. Then, begin to build it.

A good exercise at the beginning is to track all your expenses for two months. Every expense. This is not as arduous as it sounds, thanks to technology. Where is your money going? There are tools like Credit Karma and free apps from your bank to help you track your spending. This benchmark — real data showing where your money is actually going — is the first step to help you determine where you have room to save. Two months are better than one because of a rare expense or two that might skew the average during any particular month.

You can start small — as in, find a lower-price bottle of wine you like, instead of paying $15 or $20 a bottle. Trader Joe's Charles Shaw brand at $3 per bottle isn't bad at all — and a case of it costs less than some individual bottles that don't necessarily taste better. Trader Joe's has other great values that can add up to significant savings on your groceries — without feeling like scrimping. You can always splurge. But just like losing weight, if you can pare back your habitual consumption mildly, it makes all the difference in the long run.

On the fashion front, discounters carry lots of terrific basic items at a fraction of the price you can pay elsewhere. Without dropping thousands online or inside the chic retailer of choice, you can still look great and have fun shopping without burning a forest of green.

In a workshop I led on building financial security, one middle-aged woman said that when she saw a cute clothing item for a baby, she had to buy it. She didn't know why. She didn't have children. She didn't have grandchildren. But she was compelled. While some of the purchases became gifts, other tiny onesies and miniature dresses simply piled up in her house. Another woman said whenever she bought potato chips, she bought three bags instead of one. There was no reason for purchasing multiples. But when she ate two bags instead of one, she was sorry. Some of us stock up our pantries because it makes us feel secure. None of these habits is fatal, but observe the patterns and try to understand what's driving your behavior. If you realize you're spending a lot of money buying things you don't need, that consciousness alone is the first step to breaking a destructive pattern. Make small adjustments, not radical cuts in spending, to create sustainable habits.

Saving money doesn't have to be a chore. Think of it as a challenge or a game. The goal is finding creative ways to reduce spending but continue to enjoy life. Once you adjust your habits to use your money more wisely, you will feel a sense of satisfaction and start to see growth in your bank account.

How much money should you have in savings for a rainy day? Some people say keep a four-month cashflow. I say, "Why stop there?" It goes without saying, you should max out on the retirement savings benefits your organization offers. You should be deducting the maximum possible for your 401K/IRA. Why? This money goes into savings without being taxed. Your employer usually matches some part of your savings to incentivize you. Save the maximum allowed. And then save more.

Good Debt vs. Bad Debt

Just about everyone uses debt. Our economy relies on it. Debt and financing are like oxygen in our economy. We need to use debt to have credit cards, to buy a house, maybe to attend college, or to own a car.

But there is a difference between "good debt" and "bad debt."

In general, low-interest, longterm debt like a home mortgage is "good debt," and higher interest debt such as credit card debt is "bad debt." You want to take advantage of the former and stay away from the latter.

Let's talk about mortgage debt. Buying a property with mortgage debt — which for most Americans is the only way to buy a home — allows you to make a valuable investment that typically grows in value over the course of the mortgage. If mortgage rates are high, consider your timing. It may make sense to wait.

No matter what the interest rate, if you take on a mortgage, you end up paying major sums of money in interest to the lender. Here is an example. You buy a house for $300,000, with a 20 percent down payment of $60,000. You take out a $240,000 30-year fixed rate mortgage at a 3.52% interest rate. Over the course of the mortgage, you will actually pay $574,821 including $334,821 in interest. That's $334,821 you will pay to the bank! Why would you do that?

Well, you needed the loan to buy the house. But you are NOT stuck with that $334,821 interest bill. Why? You can choose a shorter term loan. A 15-year mortgage leaves you with $148,293.81 in interest to pay — that's less than half of a 30-year mortgage. And your monthly mortgage payment is not significantly higher. Forcing yourself to pay a higher monthly payment means more savings for you. Some call it "forced saving" because the principal portion of your payment is *your* money — in the form of equity.

Also, make sure you secure a mortgage with no pre-payment penalty. That way, you can pay off the mortgage early, and save the interest — your money — that would have gone to the bank. Any money paid against the principal reduces the amount of interest you will pay to the bank. So when you're tempted to blow $500 online shopping, think about the financial benefits of contributing that $500 toward your mortgage and effectively earning interest on that sum! You can consider such a contribution *earning* interest, because you won't be *paying* interest on the mortgage debt you just wiped away. When you make extra mortgage payments, instruct the bank to credit them as "principal only" payments. Doing so will reduce the amount of interest you owe. Chances are, you need the money more than the bank!

Credit Cards and Credit Scores

There are strategies to use with credit cards, too.

First, you absolutely need to pay your full credit card balance every month by the due date. But did you know that if you keep your credit card balance low by paying down your balance over the course of the month before the due date, your credit score will start to rise — significantly? The higher your credit rating, the easier it will be to get good mortgage rates and secure low-cost financing in general. By contrast, if you run large credit card balances — even if you pay on time — your credit score will suffer, and the lowest interest rates may not be available to you.

"Graduates, faculty, parents, creditors . . ."

cartoonstock.com

Working on raising your credit score will save you money in the future and may be used as a qualifying factor when you're trying to rent a home. These days, employers sometimes check your credit rating during the hiring process. There is no escaping your credit score, so you might as well be proactive in managing it. The three credit bureaus are Experian, Equifax and Transunion. Each tracks your score, and may report a score that is different from the others. Contact them and find out. Free services like Credit Karma can track your score and also help you track your spending. Know your score, monitor it, pay down your debt and credit cards, and watch your credit rating ascend.

Student Debt

I become angry when I think about the number of young people saddled with debt. US student loan debt is now the second highest consumer debt category — just behind mortgage debt — and higher than aggregate credit card and auto loan debt. [36] The average federal student loan debt balance is $37,717, while the total average balance (including private loan debt) may be as high as $40,505.[37] In 2023, 43.6 million Americans have federal student debt. In total, the US has more than $1.77 trillion in outstanding student debt. Two and a half million borrowers have debts of $100,000 or more.

I could rant about this scandal, this *scam* — the fact that colleges hiked their tuitions as student loans became ubiquitous, leaving millions of students with the need to borrow more to get advanced degrees because the bachelor's became ubiquitous, almost as common as a high school diploma. This debacle was created by government policies that launched a financing orgy with huge benefits to the banking industry, leaving a crushing burden on students, their families, and the economy. Excessive student debt can delay the saving and investing young people need to do to become fully functioning adults with access to credit, the ability to buy a home, and the means to live independently.

But once you have debt, the only way to get rid of it is to pay it down. Thus, back to the savings habit — a dollar saved is better than a dollar earned. Make extra payments on your student debt, and you are effectively earning interest on those payments. Don't be discouraged — even $10 each month will add up!

The smallest Starbucks drink costs about $4 by the time you pay tax. If you save that $4 every day, five days a week, you'll end up with an extra $1,040 per year. "If you start investing that $1,040 in a Roth IRA — a retirement account funded with after-tax dollars — starting at age 25 with the goal of retiring at age 65, you could turn those undrunk coffees into $207,000," according to Ian Krietzberg of investor publication TheStreet.com. [38]

Saving as much as you can from your income is not only a short-term cushion against the inevitable bumps in a career, it is your path to independence. The fact is that financial freedom is the foundation of other benefits, including less stress and more contentment in modern life. And you can get there with small steps. Hold off on a shoe purchase, cook dinner instead of burning money on DoorDash, cut back on Starbucks, cancel a streaming subscription, buy clothes at a discounter or consignment shop.

Putting money in your bank account is investing in yourself, taking steps down the road to a better life. Tip: avoid debt in the first place! Saving first is much easier than digging out of debt later.

Do the Hustle!

Mikaela had been working for a few years after college as a graphic designer in Buffalo, New York, when she decided to visit her dad on Vieques, an island off Puerto Rico, for a few months. At 27, Mikaela needed some time to figure out her next career steps. Helping her dad renovate his house overlooking the beautiful waters of the Caribbean, Mikaela worked part-time jobs in a restaurant and in a home goods store. Despite her long hours, she loved the relaxed pace of life on the island, time in the sun, the gentle breezes that made the island's palm fronds dance. But in September, 2017, Hurricane Maria, the worst hurricane in the island's history ravaged the island, ripping roofs off houses, scattering palm trees like pixie sticks, and turning streets into gushing rivers of mud. The island was without electricity for months.

Despondent over the destruction, the owner of the home goods store in which Mikaela worked suddenly left the island and returned to Florida. The owner said that if Mikaela kept the store open, she could sell the inventory and keep the earnings. All of a sudden, Mikaela was in charge of a shop full of artsy pottery, cute towels, kitchen gadgets, and tableware. Despite the lack of electricity, flooded streets and shuttered stores that would take months or years to re-open, Mikaela enjoyed being her own boss. Her artistic talent led to a knack for dining table decor. She changed the window displays and gave discounts to friends to encourage a trickle of customers and word of mouth. Mikaela liked setting her own hours and the ability to flex her creative muscles. She was good at bookkeeping and liked talking with neighbors and tourists who wandered into the store.

cartoonstock.com

One day, Mikaela noticed that a large space across the street was for rent. The storefront was inside a beautiful historic structure with a cathedral tin roof and ceramic-tiled floors.

Given that Vieques was in recovery, the town's coffee shops were all shuttered. Mikaela recognized both a need and an opportunity. Islanders needed coffee and the community gathering spot that a local café provides. She loved the social aspect of running the housewares store and envisioned combining the housewares and gift sales with a café. Lots of work would be required to turn the new space into her dream, but her dad and friends offered to help.

Saying a prayer, Mikaela signed the lease. Her dad helped her with carpentry, building a huge wooden table as a centerpiece, and renovating the open space. Soon, The Rising Roost Café was open for business. Importing supplies onto the island, given the hurricane recovery, was a challenge. Mikaela would make trips to the mainland every other week to buy essentials at Walmart — the trip was more reliable than waiting for shipments, even with a minimalist menu.

One day, Joseph, a FEMA disaster relief coordinator, came into the shop. He ordered an espresso. Mikaela apologized, explaining that an espresso machine was on order. "If you don't have espresso, you're not serving coffee," Joseph said, teasing her. A few weeks later, the espresso machine arrived, and Joseph returned to the store. He became a regular, enjoying the espresso. He liked The Rising Roost. Then, he fell in love with Mikaela. They married and ran the café together until their first child, Eva, was born in 2019.

Despite the challenges of running a business on an island off the coast of Puerto Rico, A Mikaela exclaimed, "I love my life!" Her mom came to visit during the winter and helped at the Rising Roost. Mikaela has never looked back on her decision to leave her graphic design job in snowy Buffalo. "What seemed like a big risk at the time turned out to be one of the best decisions I ever made," Mikaela says.

A short ferry ride from Vieques, just a few miles northeast on the island of Culebra, you might see South African-born Clive at the hardware store or watching the harbor from his roof terrace, sipping dark roast coffee as the sky explodes into purple, orange, and pinks at sunrise. Clive worked for 20 years as chief financial officer for the largest investment bank in the world, JP Morgan Chase. "My job was fixing businesses, turning them into major profit centers. If you were growing a business 10% a year, it was my job to kill it, or figure out if it could generate double and triple returns," Clive said. "I was paid to be an asshole."

cartoonstock.com

Ready for a change after two decades of investment banking, Clive took a retirement package at age 50 and started investing in and turning businesses around, including a gelato company and a novel sustainable fish farming operation. Then, a single moment changed his life forever. Clive's mitral valve exploded, forcing a multiple bypass operation on his heart. "I discovered that stress was like cancer," he said. In 2013, Clive and his wife Margaret bought a dilapidated structure on the tiny island off the coast of Puerto Rico, where he now owns and manages several Airbnbs. "Like before, I can't sit still, but I don't stress about anything," he said.

Clive loves working with guests. Recently, he comforted Airbnb visitors who had to be rerouted a few times on the erratic island ferry service. "I'm so sorry this happened to you," he soothed. "They're stupid in the ticket offices. They're bureaucrats." He went on to suggest an alternative ferry route and picked up the guests in his SUV late at night, delivering them to the Airbnb.

Clive delights his guests with the polished manners he learned in the executive suites of London high finance, making them feel like royalty. But now, dressed in a well-worn T-shirt instead of a Brioni suit, wearing a three-day-old scruff, he doesn't worry about shareholders and backstabbers in the rat race. His days are spent painting, doing light carpentry, bringing back a neglected, faded villa to its original majesty.

Quality Time

You don't have to start an ambitious business to make money. Gino retired from the pharmaceutical industry and moved to the west coast of Florida. He walks dogs to earn pocket money. He loves it. "I miss my friends, but I love my lifestyle here," he tells a visitor.

Gino has made a lot of new friends.

Kennedy was the marketing design chief at a global nonprofit for 13 years. She was responsible for the look of the nonprofit's graphics, website, design themes, supervising a broad team. When a new CEO came in, she hired a VP of Marketing who became Kennedy's boss. "Jack" had come from the advertising agency world, and loved talking about ideas, but rarely responded to emails or answered questions from Kennedy and other direct reports. The VP was brought in to "shake things up" but didn't seem to want to manage the team. Kennedy found herself working longer hours, trying to answer colleagues' questions, and becoming more and more frustrated. Strands of her dark brown curly hair started to turn gray, then fall out. "Unless you said things that went along with him, you couldn't even use your own brain. You had to play up to him," she said.

One day, Jack told Kennedy she was no longer needed at the nonprofit, and she should clear out her desk and leave at the end of the next week. Kennedy was stunned. She had built the creative team and loved the work and her colleagues. Jack said she would get one month of severance because the nonprofit didn't have money for more. The months of increasing frustration had taken a toll on Kennedy. Her friends and family told her she looked depleted, almost ill. She felt crummy.

"It really was painful. For the first few weeks, I was an emotional wreck. I asked a friend to come over while I folded my laundry. I couldn't sleep. I had an incredible amount of anxiety and fear," Kennedy, having just turned 50, reported. "One morning I called a friend at 6:00 in the morning, I was so worked up," Kennedy admitted.

The fear of not working, of running out of money — even though she had enough savings to sustain her for at least a year — sent waves of stress vibrating through her body. To calm herself, Kennedy started going to a local pottery studio she had visited in the past. She began spending hours almost daily with the clay, getting her strength back. She exercised for the first time in months. Finally, she could face the prospect of looking for work.

"I immediately started calling people with whom I had worked with before, letting them know that I was available." Soon, Kennedy attracted freelance assignments lasting days or weeks. "Not a full rush of projects, but the work came in." Kennedy pursued her freelance assignments in the morning and spent afternoons in the pottery studio. "I wanted to get better at something, to build my confidence back up," Kennedy said, her now thick, brown curls falling over her eyebrows.

Kennedy moved out of her large apartment and rented a room from a friend. "My lease was up, and I didn't want the stress of a large rental payment every month," she said. "I still had fun and did stuff, but I was really careful about spending money after I was fired." Kennedy estimates that she spent $12,000 of her savings in the 18 months she was freelancing.

Then, the universe offered up a great reward. Kennedy was offered a job as creative director at a small marketing firm where a friend worked. In fact, the firm created a new position especially for her. The new role was a dream come true, Kennedy said. And when she looked at her finances of the past year, she realized she had earned more money — after taxes and paying for her own health insurance — than she ever did in a year at the nonprofit. "If I had known that would be the case, I would have quit years ago!" Kennedy said. "I'm now making 20-30 percent more than I did in my previous job. I'm in a place where I am respected and valued. It is a marketing firm full of leaders who have worked at top companies like Apple. The caliber of my colleagues is incredible. And they're terrific to work with."

Starting your own business is not for everyone, but can be an excellent alternative whether as your main pursuit, as a side gig, or as temporary employment while you seek a permanent role. Financial resources including loans from the U.S. Small Business Administration, sites like GoFundme.com, and nonprofit lenders such as Accion Opportunity Fund abound.

Top Ten Reasons To Start Your Own Business

1. Each day at the office will be motivating.
2. You'll be following your passions.
3. You can pursue social justice.
4. You can achieve financial independence.
5. You can control your lifestyle and schedule.
6. You can start from scratch.
7. You'll get tax benefits.
8. You will have true job security.
9. You will become an expert at a broad range of skills.
10. You can be creative.

Source: Accion Opportunity Fund

Dr. Marilyn Smith (her real name), started a business almost by accident late in her high-flying career. "I'm the Word Smith. I coach people who are typically writing books," Marilyn says. "Part of the coaching is helping them lay out what they want to write about, helping them move forward — whatever they need. This afternoon I read a chapter of one of my client who has twins with bipolar disorder. This chapter was about the emotional toll on him." Marilyn has coached authors writing on a broad range of topics. The published works she has edited stretch a yard across her bookshelf.

Marilyn's new career wasn't planned. "I have an immune health problem. In my 50s, I was sick all the time because everyone came to work sick. At 60 I had to leave my job," she said. Out of work and seeking intellectual stimulation, the former national nonprofit leader signed up for a class at The Writer's Center, in Bethesda, Maryland. Marilyn wrote a memoir which was so well received, the center asked her to *teach* memoir writing. Then Marilyn developed new classes for students. Budding authors hired her to coach them on the side. Finally, a friend suggested, "You ought to start a business."

The PhD had a storied career behind her, including leading a state agency and testifying before Congress, but consulting and coaching satisfied her in ways the corporate and government worlds couldn't. "When the pandemic came, everyone wanted to write. I had clients in Liberia, Brazil," she said, green eyes sparkling through her tortoise-framed reading glasses. The business took off.

"A couple of things made this work," she adds. "I didn't need benefits. I receive Social Security and Medicare. It's not like I'm living off the money I make. What I earn as the Word Smith is my travel fund," Marilyn emphasizes. Her work, she said, "is very satisfying. I think about stopping it now that I have a new partner, but he works, too," she said. "This is an example of turning lemons into lemonade."

Marilyn has gone through the hellfire of being terminated. "It was *the* most humiliating moment in my life," she said. In typical modern executive firing fashion, the navy-suited, pump-wearing CEO was escorted out of the building as her shocked staff watched, jaws dropping. The experience stretched her. "You can always find ways to land on your feet," she said.

Financial guru Dave Ramsey's website Ramsey Solutions offers a list of 27 side hustles including tutoring online, teaching English, and renting out a room on Airbnb. "Some are quick ways to earn extra dough, and others require more time and training. But the key to winning with any side hustle is to focus on your specific skills and take advantage of them," Ramsey writes.[39]

In the increasingly transitory workplace, small businesses or "side hustles" are an excellent way to reach a savings goal, pay down student loans, build a travel fund, or add some breathing room to your budget. Side hustles are also a financial *safety net*, an insurance policy to protect you in bumpy economic times.

One of the definitions of the word "hustle" is "to induce (someone) to gamble when the odds of winning are overwhelmingly in one's own favor." The truth is, a side hustle may be a terrific way to try your hand at being an entrepreneur, make extra money, and be of service. Bet on yourself.

Looking Ahead

Technology is changing the workplace and hiring processes at warp speed. As firms rely more and more on Artificial Intelligence (AI), landing a job will require increasing attention to writing your resume to jump the technological fences to have your CV seen by real humans. Concurrently, the candidate qualification process has been infiltrated by new, technology-based screening.

"The good news is things look good. The bad news is that's just a crack in the wall."

cartoonstock.com

Aisha, an advertising executive, was asked to take a series of assessment tests by a firm considering her for a senior sales position. The tests, reminiscent of aptitude tests like the SAT or ACT, took hours to complete. "After I spoke directly with the CEO about a position, the HR department sent me several tests that took hours and hours. I've heard that companies use the tests to find out whether a candidate is really interested in a position. But it was off-putting. The hiring process has really changed."

Assessment tests measuring candidates' skills, knowledge, aptitude or personality may offer employers an inexpensive measuring tool in the hiring process, but such tests also carry risks — including bias woven into the questions, the inability of standardized tests to measure aptitude and valuable personal attributes, and losing good candidates who don't want to subject themselves to grueling online examinations. "The potential that these tools could have a discriminatory impact on certain protected classes of individuals has been the major concern related to assessment tools," said attorney Peter Cassat, a labor and employment expert at law firm Culhane Meadows in Washington, D.C., in an article published by the Society of Human Resources Management (SHRM). Many assessment tests, which have proliferated as a cost-saving method to make hiring more efficient, produce faulty results, say experts. "The risk here is wasting time and effort in using a tool that doesn't work, resulting in lower-quality candidates making it to the next step in the hiring process or being hired," Jamie Winter, vice president of talent acquisition at APTMetrics, an HR consulting firm, added in the SHRM article. [40]

Another result of proliferating technology in the hiring process is an increase in recruitment scams. So prevalent are these fraudulent schemes that U.S. Federal Trade Commission has launched an awareness campaign to protect job applicants. "Scammers advertise jobs the same way honest employers do — online (in ads, on job sites, and social media), in newspapers, and sometimes on TV and radio. They promise you a job, but what they want is your money and your personal information." The FTC's website offers a detailed guide to widespread scams, how to protect yourself, and what to do if you find yourself caught in a bogus recruitment process or "business opportunity." The Better Business Bureau (BBB) warns of a widespread resume scam: [41]

> *You're contacted by a headhunting company that found your information on LinkedIn or a job search website. They claim you are an excellent candidate for a well-paying position they are looking to fill. You must send them your resume and do a virtual interview. The request seems reasonable, so you email them your resume. Shortly afterward, they contact you letting you know they received the resume, but it isn't properly formatted for their Applicant Tracking System (ATS). Now, the "recruiter" directs you to a website where you can get the resume reformatted.*
>
> *You visit the website, where you find out you'll need to submit personal information and make a payment for the service. If you accept, you'll receive a "formatted" resume that doesn't look much different from your original resume — if you receive anything at all. The formatting service is a dishonest scheme to get your money and personal details. The job you're applying for doesn't even exist.*

ATS is real. The Better Business Bureau (BBB) recommends using traditional formatting and simple fonts to avoid snags with this widespread recruiting software. "Don't include extra colors, tables, and charts," says the BBB. "Spell out acronyms. And submit your resume as a Word doc instead of a PDF. These are easy 'fixes' you don't need to pay for." The technology age requires extra caution in sharing personal details, warns the BBB. "Don't be quick to share your details. Scammers may insist they need payment information to fix your resume or bank details to set up a direct deposit before you've even been interviewed. These are common scam tactics that put you at risk for identity theft." Searching for a job is always stressful. The digital age, while enabling employers and candidates to access unlimited opportunities, also requires extra caution, and, above all, alertness.

Fed Up to Fabulous?

What is the result of our increasing dependence on technology in the workplace? Despite wage increases, more paid time off and greater control over where they work, the number of U.S. workers who said they are angry and stressed have hit record levels, as measured by the 2023 Gallup State of the Workplace Report. [42] Meanwhile, a study of 57,000 workers by consulting firm BambooHR found that job satisfaction scores have fallen to their lowest point since early 2020, after a 10 percent drop in 2023 alone. "People chafe against being micromanaged back to offices, yet they also find isolating aspects of hybrid and remote work," said *The Wall Street Journal* in an article on the topic. [43]

"One factor is the share of workers who are relatively new to their roles after record levels of job-switching," the *Journal* reported, citing a survey of 37,000 workers by software firm Qualtrics. "The upshot is that the newest workers are among the least satisfied, Qualtrics data show — a reversal of the higher levels of enthusiasm that fresh hires typically voice." What happened to the honeymoon phase? "[Technology-enabled] long distance relationships between bosses and staff might also be an issue," the *Journal* reported. "Nearly a third of workers at large firms don't work in the same metro area as their managers, up from about 23 percent in February 2020, according to data from payroll provider ADP," the article continued. "Distance has weakened ties among coworkers and heightened conflict," said Moshe Cohen, a mediator and negotiation coach who teaches conflict resolution at Boston University's Questrom School of Business. He has noticed more employees calling coworkers or bosses "toxic or impossible, signs that trust is thin." [44]

In the Gallup report, six in ten employees said that they are "quiet quitting," a phenomenon borne of the COVID pandemic. "Quiet quitting is what happens when someone psychologically disengages from work. They may be physically present or logged into their computer, but they don't know what to do or why it matters. They also don't have any supportive bonds with their coworkers, boss or their organization," said Gallup. More than half of all workers, 51 percent, are actively or passively looking for a new job, Gallup found. [45]

While somewhat shocking, these findings are not surprising. The pleasure of the workplace, for most us, has always stemmed from a feeling of camaraderie with our colleagues, or the gratification of being appreciated for work contributed, and often, longtime friendships formed during the course of one's career. In short, the positive human exchange resulting from schlepping to the office every day. As much as people detest long commutes, is it possible that the isolation caused by technology is worse? Technology offers many benefits, and many challenges. As employers try to balance goals like productivity, financial results and employee retention, many workplace policies are in flux. A certain permanent unpredictability at work may be the result. That said, technologies (consider the wheel, the typewriter, the telephone) have always made the workplace simultaneously challenging and exciting. Adaptation is the key. Beyond the daily tacking and jibing necessary to survive at work — now and long into the future — how will we thrive?

Reflections

Once on a date with a guy who poked fun at my resume's many zigs and zags, I bragged that I would *never* be dismissed from the CEO position I held at the time. "They won't fire m e," I crowed, flinging the back of my hand at the air to wave away his preposterous thinking. "I'm too competent! The organization has been turned around. The board knows what a good job the team and I are doing." A few months later, I was handed walking papers and told to pack up my desk! Ouch.

Why was I fired so many times? The reasons, I think, boil down to a combination of inexperience and my erroneous belief that if I worked hard and "did the right thing" in every situation, I would not only succeed, but be protected from the typical attacks and petty assaults that breed in most workplaces. Hard work, integrity and commitment, I thought, would form a shield around me, deflecting spears hurled due to envy, insecurity, and fear.

I was wrong. Not only did I make serious mistakes due to lack of experience, but I was punished in several situations for conducting myself correctly. Specifically, reporting sexual harassment, discrimination, and misconduct by managers landed me on the sidewalk a few times. Acting honorably — even courageously — led directly and unequivocally to multiple ousters. One more *heads up*, high achievers: Stealthy workplace jealousy guarantees that knives are drawn when you earn attention and praise that others think *they* deserve.

How did the rest of the team respond to your promotion?

cartoonstock.com

I was very confident in myself. My self-esteem was generally high. Sometimes, my self-confidence blinded me to adversarial forces organizing around me. In other cases, I suspect my confidence squeezed out useful self-awareness of my own weaknesses and vulnerabilities. Thus, in a handful of situations, I walked confidently into buzz-saws, and was promptly let go.

But. While getting fired was humiliating, frightening, shocking, and embarrassing, the benefits were incalculable. Walking through professional flames made me stronger. Fighting the good fight built friendships of steel. The most frustrating fiascos produced lifelong supporters whose help did much more to advance my career than the terminations hindered me. You could argue that getting fired propelled my career forward. And far more numerous than the jealous vipers were bosses and colleagues who embraced, praised, and advanced my work.

I should add, I worked hard. In one job, I was *that* person who dashed into the office on Thanksgiving morning to shoot a few emails that seemed important. (*Cringe!*) In some organizations, such behavior might be discouraged — perhaps considered rude — but in my experience, energy, commitment, and motivation at work were rewarded with opportunity and advancement.

Commitment is key, says book editor and former senior executive Marilyn Smith. "I started out as a third grade teacher, so how did I end up on Capitol Hill?" she begins. "It's how you deal with circumstances. At the end of the day, it's hard work. *You have to put in the hard work.*" This may seem obvious or preachy, but in an era in which "work-life balance" has become religion, Marilyn's words are salient.

The rewards of fulfilling work can include the chance to travel, to meet interesting people, to grow and contribute — all while building a solid financial foundation that equals freedom. In my case, it helped that I was single during the bulk of my career. No kids at home to worry about, no sharing duties with a spouse. But regardless of your life circumstances, hard work is essential to propelling you up the career ladder.

Beyond excelling in your day-to-day duties, it is critical that you help other people on *their* career paths. Why? When you help people, you are contributing into a karmic bank account. You're building a store house of good will by giving your time and attention to others.

One of the downstream benefits is that when you need help, people are there for you. In the worst moments of my career, usually after losing yet another job, I was stunned and extremely heartened to find support from so many colleagues and contacts. "Of course we can meet for coffee, Beth!" was the typical response when I asked for help during those fraught times. "Where and when?"

An even bigger benefit of helping people is that when you lend a hand to someone, *YOU* feel good. If you know someone who has lost their position or is looking for a job, proactively reach out to assist. You may not have much actual power to affect their job search, but making an effort provides a huge emotional boost.

Why? The biggest challenge people face during job transitions — especially after a firing — is a loss of confidence. And as time passes, the more they *need* confidence, many job seekers feel it slipping away, like air leaking from a balloon. As a job search wears on, self-esteem is harder to maintain. The longer someone is out of a job, the greater the liability the gap can become. Unemployment can then perpetuate unemployment.

Consider Renato, a young nonprofit fundraiser, who found himself among the long-term unemployed:

"Generally, I found myself experiencing diminishing returns as my job search wore on. In one instance, a hiring manager told me that he had 'thousands of experienced people with M.A.s looking for work' and then bluntly asked me 'what made me different.' I did not bring much confidence into an interview I had at a think tank later that afternoon. My heightened self-doubt hurt my chances of being hired. It took several interactions with attentive, considerate, and thoughtful connections for me to regain the confidence that had been gradually lost." When I spoke with Renato a day or two after he first approached me, I didn't feel I had been of much help. But months later, he told me that our conversation shifted his attitude. Two job offers followed. Renato has been successfully employed — and moving up the compensation ladder — ever since.

Immediately after losing his entry-level position with a political pollster, Antony came to a networking happy hour I hosted. When I finally caught up to say hello to him at the end of the evening, Antony asked if he could take a selfie with me to post on LinkedIn. Weeks later, he said, "That happy hour was a turning point for me in my job search." I was surprised. "Why?" I asked Antony. "There were so many impressive people in that room," he recalled. "C-suite people from different organizations. There was a woman who founded an organization to help women CEOs. People from big companies. It reminded me that people are willing to help each other out here. That gives hope to people who've lost a job."

Meeting people he viewed as successful boosted Antony's confidence significantly. Within three months, he was hired by the operations team of a winning political campaign headquarters, having held temporary assignments that kept him going until he landed that position.

It's a good idea to contribute regularly, if not daily, to your karmic bank account. Here are a few specific ways you can help other people navigate, build their networks, and advance professionally:

- Invite an acquaintance to a professional event (a lecture, a networking event, etc.) he or she might find interesting.
- Endorse your contacts' skills on LinkedIn. People value recommendations. Promote your contacts' social media posts. Because we all rely on social media, helping your contacts by

promoting them in this way is truly valuable.

- Share news articles and job postings with colleagues via email and text. People appreciate that you thought of them in this simple way.
- When you are asked to meet an acquaintance about their career, try to say yes. You may not want to, but find the time. Ask to see a resume in advance. If you can, peruse the resume to capture the basics of the person's background. Schedule at least 30 minutes. It's hard to delve into a meaningful conversation if everyone is watching the clock.
- Listen actively and compassionately. Most people feel vulnerable when they are in transition. Talking about how and why they left their last job can be embarrassing. As we know from being there ourselves, transition can be very stressful.
- As you are listening, try to get a sense of the skills and interests of the person, asking questions along the way. "What do you want to do?" "What kind of organizations are you exploring?"
- If you identify cosmetic errors on a resume of a colleague in transition, speak up! As people use different versions of resumes, and as the internet age weakens grammar and writing standards, mistakes occur. You can do a huge favor for someone in transition by pointing out punctuation and spelling errors.
- Because the vast majority of jobs are filled through connections and referrals, every job seeker needs to speak with people in the workforce who might be a future source of a job or knowledge of a job. As a rule of thumb, I try to make two introductions for people who come to me for help. I always ask permission from

my contacts before making these connections. I can't think of a time anyone has said "no." After making an introduction, feel free to exit the exchange.

- People may forget to thank you even after benefiting from introductions to your contacts. Don't worry about it. By fostering new connections and networking conversations, you successfully deposited in your karmic bank account.

Beyond taking direct steps to help others who are looking for opportunities, the following simple practices will make *your* day in the workplace better:

- Say "thank you" — more than once — to anyone who helps you in any way.
- Look for ways to compliment people. Everyone needs a lift. It doesn't cost a thing!
- Each day, smile! Lift both corners of your mouth, especially when you are feeling low or blah. You can literally change a moment or a whole day by smiling. Exercise those muscles. The world will respond!

In an article in the *Harvard Business Review* titled, "When Getting Fired Is Good for Your Career," Elena Lytkina Botelho wrote, "More than 20 years of advising and coaching leaders has shown us that when you try to achieve something meaningful, you'll face blow-ups from time to time. What matters more, is that you address the failure as an opportunity for growth. It can be a real travesty when, by playing defense throughout their careers, so many of us miss a chance to grow to our full potential and to live more meaningful lives. In the words of Oliver Wendell Holmes, 'Many people die with their music still in them.'" [46]

Whether you've been fired, passed over, or pushed aside, you are well positioned to regroup, re-invent, and relaunch. You are officially ready to reach the next peak of your life. Work hard, smile, and help others. Your ascent begins now.

Acknowledgements

A few exceptions notwithstanding, my career brought me into the orbit of truly awesome bosses and mentors. It's impossible to properly thank the great leaders I have worked for and with, but, to all of you, I owe the thanks of a lifetime.

To Andy Alexander, Jim Amos, Fredrick Anyanwu, Ted Balestreri, Rep. Mike Barnes, Lina Bonova, Steve Caldeira, Andre Carothers, Tom Cator, Dick Crawford, Lauren Crawford, Jeanne Cummings, Didi Cutler, LeeAnn Dance, Janet Donovan, Dina Dwyer-Owens, Gov. John Engler, Joe Fassler, Ross Fineman, Michèle Flournoy, Page Gardner, Jeff Gedmin, Andy Glass, Cindy Grande, Bill Hall, John Hamre, Mayor Teresa Heitmann, Gary Honig, Bob Hurt, Bill Isaac, Steve Joyce, Frank X. Keane, Peter Kelley, Earl Klitenic, Jim Malone, Dick Marriott, Dean McGrath, Ken Moffett, Abigail Lewis, Michael Meehan, Rep. Jim Moran, Rep. Connie Morella, Adm. Mike Mullen, Colleen Nunn, Michelle Nunn, Sen. Sam Nunn, Jim Perna, Gen. Arnold Punaro, Bill Rice, Kiki Sahl, Didi Schanche, Todd Shields, Bill Schweitzer, Mary Kennedy Thompson, Jay Timmons, Jeff Trandahl, Lynda Webster, Mayor Anthony Williams, and last, but never, ever least, Philip Zeidman.

THANK YOU!!!

A special thanks to "The Word Smith," Dr. Marilyn Smith, who skillfully edited and patiently polished this manuscript so it could shine. Thanks to cheakina on fiverr.com for designing this book ingeniously from cover to cover, and to cartoonstock.com and Glasbergen Cartoon Service for permission to use the jolly illustrations herein. A shoutout to Ellie Maranda at Politics & Prose for quickly getting up to speed and taking us over the finish line.

The support of my beloved Gero, as well as my brother Harrison, niece Jessie and nephews Sam and James, and fellow writer and nephew Leander Geilenbruegge, kept the wind beneath my wings during the years required to finish this book. Thank you for your love and endless support!

From Fired to Fabulous is the result of generous contributions by many friends, family and colleagues, who shared their stories, offered encouragement, and gave their precious time. My heartfelt thanks to: Amb. Abdulwahab Alhajjri, Emily Baker, Marguerite Benson-West, Lynly Boor, Brad Brown, Alison Cardy, Andre Carothers, Francesca Craig, Letitia Crawford, Dana Daoud, David and Marilyn Einhorn, Joern and Monika Erdmann, Sherry Ettleson, Katie Fischer Crisalli, Tobias Froehlich, Sona Gandhi, Arno and Christiane Geilenbruegge, Ivo and Kirsten Geilenbruegge, Tessa Geilenbruegge, Karen Gold, Ari Goldberg, Colleen Groves, Claudia and Wolfram Irmer, Valerie Kirkpatrick, Kate Lehrer, Diane McDonnell, Margaret McDonnell, Joe Minatulo, Melanie Minzes, Robie Mitchell, Rachel Mlinarchik, angel-in-real-life Colleen Nunn, Kojo Otchere, Adrian Palau, Alex Ruttenberg, Ann Pincus, Richard Rogers, Vicki Simarano, Kathy Smith, Lauren Supina, Dean and Ray Turner, and Clive Zickel. You are the best!

Endnotes

1 *PBS Newshour*, Sept. 2018

2 "Employees who stay in companies longer than two years get paid 50 percent less," Forbes.com, Oct. 2014

3 "Social Trends," Pewresearch.org, July 2022

4 Careercontessa.com

5 "Four Ways to Control Your Emotions in Tense Moments," by Joseph Genny, HBR.com, July 2016

6 Alison can be reached at www.cardycareercoaching.com

7 HBR.com, Oct. 2018

8 *AARP Magazine*, Jan. 2020

9 *Weekend Edition*, NPR, Oct. 2019

10 *Vanity Fair*, Nov. 2019

11 The *David Rubenstein Show*, Bloomberg News, March 1, 2017

12 Burt Reynolds on day he and Clint Eastwood were fired, "Rewind," take2markTV, Nov. 2021

13 *Bird by Bird*, by Anne Lamott, Knopf Doubleday, 1995

14 *Coach Yourself to a New Career*, by Talane Miedaner, McGraw Hill, 2010

15 *Grit, The Power of Passion and Perseverance*, by Angela Duckworth, Simon & Schuster, 2016

16 "The Class of 2023 Faces a Jittery Job Market: 'The World Seems to Have Flipped on Its Head,'" by Lindsay Ellis and Kailyn Rhone, *The Wall Street Journal*, March 2023

17 *Switchers*, by Dawn Graham, AMACOM, 2018

18 *Switchers*, by Dawn Graham, AMACOM, 2018

19 Forbes.com, Dec. 2018

20 Indeed.com, April 2023

21 "What not to Wear to a Job Interview," by Francesca Fontana, *The Wall Street Journal*, January 6, 2024

22 Ibid.

23 MuchSkills.com, 2023

24 "Is Gen Z the boldest generation? Its job-hunt priorities are off the charts," LinkedIn.com, Feb. 2022

25 Voya.com, Sept.2020

26 *Squawk Box*, CNBC.com, July 2023

27 Monthly Labor Review, BLS.gov, 2018-2028

28 SSA.gov

29 Resumebuilder.com, May 2023

30 "Why Reverse Mentoring Works, and How to do it Right," HBR.com, October 2019

31 Investopedia.com, March 2023

32 EEOC.gov

33 Investopedia.com, March 2023

34 LinkedIn.com, Feb. 2023

35 *Badass Habits*, by Jen Sincero, Penguin Life 2020

36 McKinsey & Co., April 2020

37 Education Data Initiative, 2023

38 "Can Skipping Your Daily Starbucks Really Ensure a Blissful Retirement? We took a look at the math," by Ian Krietzberg, The Street.com, June, 2023

39 "27 Side Hustle Ideas to Earn Extra Cash," Ramseysolutions.com, Aug. 2023

40 "Your Hiring Assessments Could Get You in Trouble," by Lin Grensing-Pophal, SHRM.org

41 https://consumer.ftc.gov/articles/job-scams

42 https://www.gallup.com/workplace/349484/state-of-the- global-workplace.aspx

43 "Grumpy on the Job? You have Company," by Vanessa Fuhrmans and Lindsay Ellis, *The Wall Street Journal*, Nov. 27, 2023

44 "Grumpy on the Job? You have Company," by Vanessa Fuhrmans and Lindsay Ellis, *The Wall Street Journal*, Nov. 27, 2023

45 45 https://www.gallup.com/workplace/349484/state-of-the- global-workplace.aspx

46 "When Getting Fired Is Good for Your Career," by Lytkina Botelho, HBR.com, Oct. 2018

Made in the USA
Middletown, DE
14 January 2025